EMPLOYMENT
of the
MIDDLE-AGED

EMPLOYMENT

of the

MIDDLE-AGED

Papers From Industrial
Gerontology Seminars

Compiled and Edited by

GLORIA M. SHATTO

Associate Professor of Economics
University of Houston
Houston, Texas

CHARLES C THOMAS • PUBLISHER
Springfield • Illinois • U.S.A.

Published and Distributed Throughout the World by
CHARLES C THOMAS • PUBLISHER
BANNERSTONE HOUSE
301–327 East Lawrence Avenue, Springfield, Illinois, U.S.A.

© 1972 by THE NATIONAL COUNCIL ON THE AGING
1828 L Street, N.W., Washington, D.C.

ISBN 0–398–02408–1

Library of Congress Catalog Card Number: 70–187677

With THOMAS BOOKS *careful attention is given to all details of
manufacturing and design. It is the Publisher's desire to present books
that are satisfactory as to their physical qualities and artistic possibilities
and appropriate for their particular use.* THOMAS BOOKS *will be true
to those laws of quality that assure a good name and good will.*

This book is a result of seminars sponsored by the National Institute
of Industrial Gerontology, a program of the National Council on the
Aging and funded in part through the Manpower Administration,
United States Department of Labor through the Minnesota Department
of Manpower Services.

HD
6280
.S5

Printed in the United States of America

BB-14

CONTRIBUTORS

RASHELLE G. AXELBANK
Consultant to the NCOA National Institute of
Industrial Gerontology
Formerly Labor Market Analyst with the
New York State Division of Employment

RICHARD E. BARFIELD, Ph.D.
Assistant Study Director
Survey Research Center
The University of Michigan
Ann Arbor, Michigan

MONROE BERKOWITZ, Ph.D.
Professor of Economics
Rutgers University
New Brunswick, New Jersey

IAN CAMPBELL
Associate Director
Manpower Utilization Branch
Department of Manpower and Immigration
Canada

SIDNEY COBB, M.D., M.P.H.
Program Director
Survey Research Center, and
Lecturer in Epidemiology
University of Michigan
Ann Arbor, Michigan

JAMES L. FOZARD, Ph.D.
Research Psychologist
Normative Aging Study
Veterans Administration Outpatient Clinic, Boston, and
Principal Research Associate in Psychiatry
Harvard Medical School
Cambridge, Massachusetts

RUSSEL F. GREEN, Ph.D.
Research Consultant, Psychology and Education
Henrietta, New York

v

LEON GREENBERG
Associate Commissioner
United States Bureau of Labor Statistics

LAWRENCE D. HABER
Director, Division of Disability Studies
Office of Research and Statistics
Social Security Administration

STANISLAV V. KASL, Ph.D.
Associate Professor of Epidemiology and Psychology
Yale University School of Medicine
New Haven, Connecticut

JUANITA M. KREPS, Ph.D.
Professor of Economics
and Dean, The Woman's College
Duke University
Durham, North Carolina

JACK A. MEYER
Research Associate
Center for Human Resource Research
Ohio State University
Columbus, Ohio

RONALD L. NUTTALL, Ph.D.
Associate Professor
Institute of Human Sciences
Boston College
Chestnut Hill, Massachusetts

CHARLES E. ODELL
Deputy Associate Manpower Administrator
United States Training and Employment Service
United States Department of Labor

HERBERT S. PARNES, Ph.D.
Research Associate
Center for Human Resource Research
Ohio State University
Columbus, Ohio

GUNARS REIMANIS, Ph.D.
Director of Research
Corning Community College
Corning, New York

THEODOR SCHUCHAT
Journalist
Washington, D.C.

HAROLD L. SHEPPARD, Ph.D.
Staff Social Scientist
The W.E. Upjohn Institute for
Employment Research

IRMA WITHERS
Deputy Director,
National Institute of Industrial Gerontology
National Council on the Aging

INDUSTRIAL GERONTOLOGY—
A DEFINITION

Industrial gerontology is the study of the employment and retirement problems of middle-aged and older workers.

Industrial gerontology begins where age becomes a handicap to employment. Age discrimination in employment may start as early as thirty-five or forty in some industries and occupations, and begins to take on major dimensions at age forty-five. Federal and state age discrimination in employment legislation generally applies to the ages forty to sixty-five.

Industrial gerontology is concerned with aptitude testing of the middle-aged and older worker, with job counseling, vocational training, and placement. It is concerned with job adjustment, assignment, reassignment, retention, motivation, and mobility. It is concerned with the transition from employment to retirement and with retirement itself. It is concerned with retirement preparation, retirement income and with public and private pension programs.

Industrial gerontology draws upon economics, psychology, medicine, sociology, adult education, industrial and labor relations, and management science.

Industrial gerontology is a new applied social science field.

NORMAN SPRAGUE
Director
National Institute of Industrial Gerontology

INTRODUCTION

Our national goal of full employment assumes new dimensions as adjustments are made for changes in retirement practices, technological innovations, and age shifts of the population. The middle-aged and older workers are receiving more attention as their special problems of long-term unemployment, involuntary retirement, and inadequate income are recognized. These mature workers, generally those forty-five and older, find that advancing age influences their ability to remain employed and when displaced their ability to find new employment.

There is a continuum of age-related employment and income problems that begin around age forty and become greater after age forty-five. Statistics on poverty in 1970 indicate that the number of elderly persons, over age sixty-five, in the poverty category is increasing. Furthermore, employment data suggest that persons over age fifty-five represent a potential future poverty group.* The size of retirement income is related to the level of employment income and the time dimension, including the continuity, of employment. To have adequate retirement income, middle-aged persons must have employment opportunities; thus, the years after age forty-five are crucial.

Training, continuing education, and counseling are as essential for the mature worker as for the new entrant to employment. Public and private employers must recognize the potential waste of human resources resulting from the unemployment of the middle-aged and revise the institutional framework to utilize fully this human capital. Maximum employment of middle-aged workers contributes to the individual well-being of these persons as well as to the economic growth of the nation.

The papers in this book analyze various aspects of employment problems and opportunities facing middle-aged and older

---

* United States Senate, Special Committee on Aging: *Developments in Aging 1970*. 92nd Cong., 1st Session, March 23, 1971, pp. 3–4.

persons. In searching for avenues to improve the income and future retirement prospects of the middle-aged, the writers explore many facets of attitudinal and financial support to identify specific supportive roles of employers, unions, employment counselors, and others. Many contributors elaborate policy objectives and suggest legislative changes in such areas as medical needs and health insurance, portable pensions, and improvements in workmen's compensation.

The first section offers justification for a special study of employment-related problems of middle-aged and older persons. Harold Sheppard examines many areas of industrial gerontology where progress can be achieved through further research and greater institutional adaptations by agencies working with the mature worker. Irma Withers describes the aging of the population over the last century. She notes that these major population changes will force society to reappraise the role assignments for various age groups. Can we continue earlier retirements, even when scientists announce new discoveries that will prolong life? Rashelle Axelbank describes trends in occupational patterns that have accompanied changes in industrial patterns. Age discrimination in the hiring process and other employment problems of mature workers, according to Axelbank, are directly related to economic progress, technological improvements, and development of private pension programs.

Leisure and retirement choices are the focus of economists' papers in the next section. Juanita Kreps argues that society can choose among various work and leisure patterns and that options are available both in the distribution of leisure and in its time-pattern. While recognizing that leisure for the entire population depends on productivity and mentioning the social alternatives competing for the productivity increase, Leon Greenberg assesses the future capabilities of the United States economy to support additional leisure time. Richard Barfield reviews the factors that enter into the worker's decision to retire voluntarily earlier than at the conventional retirement age. His survey data reveal information about the financial status of persons already retired and the factors that contribute to the retired persons' satisfaction or dissatisfaction.

Causes of unemployment and the adverse health effects resulting from unemployment are reported in two major studies. Utilizing a representative sample of middle-aged men who withdrew from the labor force, Herbert Parnes and Jack Meyer analyze the significant factors that affect the labor force participation of that age group. Their study, part of a longitudinal study, presents generalizations about the process of labor force withdrawal. Sidney Cobb and Stanislav Kasl evaluate some of the physical and mental health problems that result when men face involuntary unemployment. Men with stable work experiences were interviewed prior to a plant's closing and for two years thereafter, allowing Cobb and Kasl to document the health deterioration that accompanies unemployment.

Mental and physical capacities, their measurement, and counseling are the subjects of the following studies by psychologists. Russel Green and Gunars Reimanis reconcile some of the conflicting evidence about age-related changes in intellectual and cognitive powers. Their study confirms that the amount of formal education is a strong determinant of a person's cognitive functioning for most of his life. Their evidence that intellectual powers remain intact at least until age sixty-five provides valuable information for vocational counselors and employers. James Fozard and Ronald Nuttall offer information about the General Aptitude Test Battery (GATB) that is useful in employment counseling. The results aid the counselor in understanding the effects of differences in age and socioeconomic status on the individual's performance on the GATB.

The general assumption that chronological age and capacity losses are closely linked leads to employment practices and social attitudes that are usually unjust in individual cases. Although Lawrence Haber finds that older workers are more severely disabled by capacity losses than are younger workers, he argues that employers could adopt and modify the task requirements to fit the individual's performance and ignore chronological age; this modification would lead to a more efficient utilization of individual capabilities. Monroe Berkowitz attacks the myth that hiring older workers has the direct effect of raising the employer's workmen's compensation insurance rates.

The last section focuses on the government's role in the solution of major problems facing middle-aged and older workers. Traditionally, legislation to bring about social reform has occurred only after a long evolutionary process. Theodor Schuchat describes these evolutionary stages of social change, with examples of legislation and reforms for mature workers. Ian Campbell describes the role assumed by the Canadian government in training mature workers and in providing adequate economic security for old age. He notes that the recently adopted Government pension plans remove some obstacles that faced private employers in hiring mature workers. Charles Odell reviews programs in the United States designed to promote employment opportunities for middle-aged and older persons. He stresses the potential voting strength of the group over forty-five which, if exerted, could bring swift reform in programs and priorities.

These papers were presented at meetings of the National Institute of Industrial Gerontology in Annapolis, Maryland, and Phoenix, Arizona. The selected papers touch only a few topics in industrial gerontology and are not closely related. The unifying theme is the unique, but serious, employment and income problems of middle-aged and older workers. We hope this book will be useful to academicians and practitioners in the varied areas associated with industrial gerontology. I would like to thank Mrs. Irma R. Withers for her assistance in preparing this manuscript.

GLORIA SHATTO

CONTENTS

                                                                         Page

Contributors   v

Industrial Gerontology—A Definition—NORMAN SPRAGUE   ix

Introduction   xi

I. DIMENSIONS OF THE PROBLEM

Chapter

1. SOME CONTRIBUTIONS OF THE SOCIAL SCIENCES TO INDUSTRIAL GERONTOLOGY
   Harold L. Sheppard   5
2. POPULATION: THE VANISHING PYRAMID
   Irma Withers   13
3. THE POSITION OF THE OLDER WORKER IN THE AMERICAN LABOR FORCE
   Rashelle G. Axelbank   17

II. THE OPTIONS: EMPLOYMENT VS. LEISURE

4. LIFETIME TRADEOFFS BETWEEN WORK AND PLAY
   Juanita M. Kreps   31
5. A NOTE ON INCOME VS. LEISURE AS RELATED TO PRODUCTIVITY
   Leon Greenberg   42
6. SOME OBSERVATIONS ON EARLY RETIREMENT
   Richard E. Barfield   45

III. UNEMPLOYMENT: SURVEYS OF THE MIDDLE-AGED

7. WITHDRAWAL FROM THE LABOR FORCE BY MIDDLE-AGED MEN, 1966–1967
   Herbert S. Parnes and Jack A. Meyer   63
8. SOME MEDICAL ASPECTS OF UNEMPLOYMENT
   Sidney Cobb and Stanislav V. Kasl   87

IV. PSYCHOLOGICAL DATA AND THE IMPLICATIONS FOR COUNSELING

9. THE AGE-INTELLIGENCE RELATIONSHIP—LONGITUDINAL STUDIES CAN MISLEAD

    Russel F. Green and Gunars Reimanis 99

10. GENERAL APTITUDE TEST BATTERY SCORES FOR MEN IN DIFFERENT AGE AND SOCIOECONOMIC GROUPS

    James L. Fozard and Ronald L. Nuttall 117

V. AGE AND CAPACITY

11. AGE AND CAPACITY DEVALUATION

    Lawrence D. Haber 141

12. WORKMEN'S COMPENSATION AND THE OLDER WORKER

    Monroe Berkowitz 169

VI. GOVERNMENTAL ENCOURAGEMENT FOR THE MIDDLE-AGED

13. TRENDS IN LEGISLATION AFFECTING OLDER WORKERS: TAKING THE LONG VIEW

    Theodor Schuchat 187

14. OLDER WORKERS IN CANADA: EMPLOYMENT, TRAINING, AND RETIREMENT

    Ian Campbell 192

15. UNITED STATES GOVERNMENT PROGRAMS FOR THE MIDDLE-AGED

    Charles E. Odell 199

Name Index 211

Subject Index 213

EMPLOYMENT
of the
MIDDLE-AGED

I. DIMENSIONS OF THE PROBLEM

Chapter 1

SOME CONTRIBUTIONS OF THE SOCIAL SCIENCES TO INDUSTRIAL GERONTOLOGY

HAROLD L. SHEPPARD

What are some of the areas in the behavioral and social sciences that can contribute to the field of gerontology? The study of population, individual social behavior, cultural factors, and institutional analysis can add to our understanding of problems of the older workers. Demography includes consideration of the balance of the population structure. To cite one example, let me call attention to certain trends and policies that are often contradictory and thus create social and economic problems.

We have progressed over the last several decades in the conquest of illness and this means that we have been highly successful in *death control*. Perhaps all cultures have felt that it is good to postpone death, but it is only in recent history that we have believed it possible to postpone death and have searched for techniques to make the delay a reality. Consequently we have a booming health industry and ascribe great status to physicians. If you tie the death control movement in with the whole philosophy of ecology which requires balance, you can see that *birth* control is a necessary concomitant of death control. I am not talking solely about medicine having made it possible for old people to live longer; the reality is that our aging problem is, in large part, a result of our success in controlling infant death.

The implications of balance are apparent when we turn to labor force participation rates. We are witnessing a declining rate of labor force participation, especially among older men. In our society, a sign of progress is the growth in the number

5

of persons *not* working. Progress is related to the number of persons who have been removed from toil in the mines or in heavy industry. We have taken as an unexamined value that the sooner people retire, the better is the society. To a great extent that is true. Until recently it was very true; but now in considering certain demographic factors, we must raise several questions. Is the working population capable and willing to support those who don't work? This question concerns the *dependency ratio* that demographers talk about: For every one hundred workers, how many people (of all ages) don't work?

Will the working population willingly support an increasing number of persons, both older and younger generations, in their own households and in society generally? Even if the ratio of nonworking persons stays constant, an increase in transfer and retirement incomes for the nonworking persons still represents a growing burden on the working population.

Another question relates to the changing pattern of educational attainment. The gap between median years in school of older workers, say those fifty-five to sixty-four, and younger workers is narrowing. The highly educated young working population of today will not be as educationally disadvantaged thirty years from now as is the current generation of older workers. Thus, lack of education may not be a legitimate reason for the older workers' unemployment problems in the future.

Second, as part of that educational phenomenon, let me refer to some of our knowledge about individual social behavior. I believe that one's self-image is affected by how many years of education one has—in terms of self-confidence, expectations out of life and expectation from others. Thus in the future we can expect *less* willingness, from the older worker, to be put to pasture in a work-oriented society. In spite of all the talk about the ability of technology to produce adequately with only two percent of the population, I do not believe the notion of (and the need to) work will change dramatically. There will be a reversal of the apparent current trend toward earlier retirement, and that will call for new arrangements in total work-life patterns. I do not believe that people in their thirties and forties today (who have a high level of education compared to their parents and grandparents) will accept the status when they become fifty-five, sixty, and sixty-five that people who are *now* fifty-five, sixty, and sixty-five are forced to accept.

Let me now give an example of what I mean by *institutional analysis* as it relates to the field of industrial gerontology. The United States Employment Service is an example of an institution that has been analyzed on a micro scale. A few years ago the Upjohn Institute for Employment Research conducted a study of what unemployed workers do when they lose their jobs. The study, called *The Job Hunt*,[1] was largely financed by the Department of Labor and was based on one of the most extensive interview schedules applied to unemployed workers in the recent history of social science research.

Among the many questions asked was: "When you were looking for a job did you go to your local employment service office?" Those who said "yes" were asked a series of new questions such as: "Did the employment service refer you to an employer for a job interview?," "Did the employment service refer you to a training program?," "Did they give you any counseling?," "Did they test you?" The analysis revealed that the older worker received fewer services from the employment service than the younger workers.

Second, we found a relationship between the number of services received and the re-employment rate. There was a statistical relationship: the greater the number of services received, the higher the percentage of workers hired at a new job. One implication is that it is important for workers to get a large number of services. An older worker in our study was anyone thirty-nine and over. I am not saying that the personnel in the employment service consciously and deliberately gave fewer services to older workers. I believe that there are certain cultural factors involved, that we are unconscious of what causes us to treat various types of people differently, and that one of the key cues we use to "differentiate" in our society is

1. Sheppard, H.L., and Belitsky, A.H.: *The Job Hunt: Job-Seeking Behavior of Unemployed Workers in a Local Economy*, Baltimore, Johns Hopkins Press, 1966.

age. If we had interviewed the Employment Service personnel, I am sure they would not have been aware of what they were doing.

Robert Butler, a psychiatrist, believes that we are in a culture dominated by *ageism,* and this ageism is more subtle than is racism.[2] Today if anyone were to write in a government memo that a training program was to be restricted to members of the Caucasian race, he would have his head cut off. There are enough people in our society now who would react negatively to that. We have succeeded at least in getting racism evaluated as an unpopular and antisocial trait.

On the other hand, I suspect that if a memo from a government agency stated that a given program was intended only for those under forty-five very few people in the clearance pipeline would pick it up and say, "Oh, wait a minute, you can't do that; why use age as a criterion?" The reason is that we have incorporated ageism so effectively into our system that we don't have any conscious negative reaction against such a notion.

A few years ago, I spent an hour and a half before a Regional Manpower Advisory Committee in the mountain states, elaborating the concept that you cannot use year of birth as a predictor of job performance, just as you cannot use skin color to predict what a person will do or think, and showing a film made by the Department of Labor indicating some of the training techniques of the British psychologist Belbin, who believes you can develop special techniques for raising the learning ability of older workers. In my presentation and discussion of the film, I talked about the need to have relevant decision-making about an individual *as an individual.*

Despite that presentation, the very first comment in the discussion that followed was by a government official who said: "Everybody knows that the *average* older person has trouble learning a new skill, or can't learn a new skill at all." When you deal with *averages,* you are indulging in stereotypes; one of the contributions of the social sciences is to examine stereotypes and to test their validity.

---

2. Butler, R.N.: The effect of medical and health progress on the social and economic aspects of the life cycle. *Industrial Gerontology, No.* 2:1–9, June 1969.

Let me come to another aspect of institutional analysis. The President's *Manpower Report* states that in 1969, 10.3 percent of the participants in Manpower Development and Training Act (MDTA) programs were forty-five or over, whereas at least one-third of the long-term unemployed were in that age category. Older persons are not proportionately represented in training programs. It may be called differential treatment, prejudice, or discrimination, but the older workers are not referred to MDTA by the "gatekeepers," who may be the Employment Service or some local educational agency. Further, some Employment Service personnel believe that the employer to whom they might refer an older worker would himself discriminate against that older person; and so the personnel of the Employment Service Office hesitate to put the older job seeker through an embarrassing and disappointing experience. Another factor contributes to the older individual's employment and training failures: many older persons believe they cannot learn new skills and have a poor image of themselves. They thus "select themselves out" of a training program.

Often employers assume that older workers have less education and thus lower skill potential. Not all jobs require as much formal education as many employers and personnel directors use as a standard in their hiring practices and policies. There are many jobs that persons without a high school education could perform, but for cultural reasons we insist on a high school education. Moreover arbitrary guidelines for hiring can result from what Alfred Sauvy of France has called *administrative laziness*. It is so much easier to make decisions if you have one cue; for example, does a person have a high school education, or has he reached age sixty-five? The alternative is to look at each person individually. More specifically, one should apply some *functional tests* to see if the applicant can really do the job, regardless of his age. That takes time and money. But are we really saving money as a total society by encouraging and tolerating administrative laziness?

One of the explanations for the problem that older job-seekers have is that they have inadequate education. *That* is why they are being discriminated against, and *that* is why they are having a tougher time. Education is an important factor, of course, but there are a few case studies which show that holding education constant, *age per se* is involved in the success of unemployed workers in getting jobs. We have reexamined the data from the Packard Motor shutdown in a recent book, *Economic Failure, Alienation and Extremism.*[3] We found that age was *the* most important explanation for the failure of the ex-Packard workers to find a new job; skill was the *second* most important reason, and education had no statistical relationship to their failure to find employment.

In another study of the hard-core unemployed in Detroit, Michigan, Howard Wachtel found that out of eight possible reasons for the continued employment problem of the hard-core unemployed, age was the *fourth* most important reason.[4] A study has been done for the Department of Labor, on the layoffs among *scientists* and *technicians* in the aircraft industries in California.[5] The study revealed that age was apparently used in selecting who would be laid off, and also that age was involved in their re-employment success. Once again, it might be argued that within each group, the *lesser* qualified, lesser educated worker was at a disadvantage compared to the better qualified, better educated scientist and engineer. By better qualified, I refer to objective indices of qualification measured by such things as number of papers written, participation in scientific societies, and other contributions to the field. The researcher who did this study took those factors into consideration and found that despite the objective indices of qualification, the older scientists and professional technicians were at a disadvantage.

Although education and skill level are certainly involved, they are not the only factors involved and sometimes age *per se* is the explanation.

3. Aiken, M., Ferman, L.A., and Sheppard, H.L. Ann Arbor, University of Michigan Press, 1969.
4. Wachtel, H.: Hard-core unemployment in Detroit: Causes and Remedies. *Industrial Relation Research Association Proceedings,* 1969, pp. 233–41.
5. Loomba, R.P.: A study of the re-employment and unemployment experiences of scientists and engineers laid off from 62 aerospace and electronics firms in the San Francisco Bay area. Mimeo report from San Jose State College for the U.S. Department of Labor (n.d.).

I examined some other aspects of the relevance of age to worker behavior in the labor market and found that there are some social-psychological factors that affect the job-seeking behavior of workers.[6] When we controlled for social-psychological factors we found that age made very little difference in job-seeking behavior. The critical factor was motivation. If an unemployed man had high achievement motivation (as measured through projective tests), age was relatively unimportant as a factor in job-finding success. His achievement motivation was the critical variable. It so happens that the older the worker the less likely it is that he will have high achievement motivation. We should not jump to the conclusion that this is, therefore, inevitable, but rather ask, "Is there a target group that we know has relatively great odds of having low achievement motivation?" If so, we must counsel them to raise their achievement motivation. David McClelland at Harvard has developed techniques for actually raising achievement motivation.

Another factor involved relates to self-image. Workers differ from each other in the degree of anxiety they have about going through the job interview experience. Accordingly, in the job-seeking study we developed a scale for measuring *job interview anxiety*. We found again that age was not important, that what *was* important was the degree to which the individual had anxieties about being interviewed.

Let me conclude with another point that relates partly to demography. Many of our pension policies and our employment policies are based on the traumas created by the Depression of the 1930's. We thought we could solve the unemployment problems by redefining certain unemployed people: call them retired, and don't count them as unemployed.

I think that we are undergoing certain cultural drifts which, over time, can engender a crisis. I do not believe that it is an unmixed blessing that we continue to reduce the age of retirement. If you look at the labor force participation rate of those sixty-two to sixty-four, you find a fantastic drop in the labor force participation rate of persons in their early sixties com-

6. Sheppard, H.L.: The relevance of age to worker behavior in the labor market, *Industrial Gerontology, 1:* 1–11, 1969.

pared with the rate for the fifty-five to fifty-nine-year-olds. More than half of the men applying for Social Security benefits now are *under* the age of sixty-five. If you hear that statistic you can say, "That is great, we are now reaching our El Dorado. These people don't have to work anymore; they have been struggling in the foundries and in a lot of other back-breaking jobs, and now they can retire." Then look at the characteristics of these early retirees and you find that they are the people who can *least* afford to retire.

What happened? These are the men who have been going through the discouragement process over the five to ten years prior to reaching the age of sixty-two. They have had intermittent jobs. They grab whatever unemployment compensation they can get and then eventually exhaust these rights. When they arrive at the age of sixty-two, they grab the next straw, which is a reduced Social Security benefit at the age of sixty-two. That is virtually all the income they can count on. I think we are creating a new poverty problem without realizing it. Every year the number of persons who reach age sixty-two has been going up. "Retirement" on a small income is not necessarily a sign of progress. We should do something about those people before they reach age sixty-two.

Illness is another explanation commonly given for the drop in labor force participation among older persons. Dr. Sidney Cobb of the University of Michigan, studying the medical impact of unemployment, found that a substantial minority of persons who were laid off (typically people in their 40's, 50's, and 60's) underwent some psychosomatic changes as a result of the layoff. The odds for their getting these particular symptoms were beyond the level of chance expectation. A report on unemployed persons who say that they are "sick," lumps into one category people who got sick because they were laid off and people who quit because they were sick. I think we have to start differentiating between the two.

We have been taking too many things for granted about aging and about the inability of older persons to work and to be retrained. Our policies are based on serious misconceptions and lack of information. Re-examination of our policies and personal attitudes is in order.

Chapter 2

POPULATION: THE VANISHING PYRAMID

IRMA WITHERS

T he population explosion is not solely attributable to baby booms; more of us are around longer. Short-run forecasts of the age structure of the population and of the labor force sometimes tend to obscure the long-term trend toward an even age distribution in the United States. The changing shape of the national age pattern is evident at a glance in Figure 2–1, which is adapted and reproduced from a United States Census Bureau report.[1]

A century ago, when both birth rates and mortality rates were high, children and young people predominated in the population. Immigration of the young from Europe also contributed to the broad base of persons under twenty-years-old in the 1870 age pattern. At that time the population, when divided into ten-year age brackets, formed a perfect pyramid.

The effect of the low birth rates that prevailed during the depression of the thirties may be observed in the 1940 pattern of age distribution; the base of the pyramid had become constricted. By 1960, however, the post-World War II increase in births had caused in the younger ages almost a reversion to the 1870 pattern. Nevertheless, the proportions in the middle and older age groups remained high because of increased longevity of the population.

In 1969 the pyramid population pattern was on the way out. The sizeable proportion of young persons in the population in that year was attributable essentially to the large number of women of child-bearing age (born after World War II)

1. United States Bureau of the Census: *Current Population Reports*, Series, P-25, 441, Estimates of the Population of the United States, by Age, Race, and Sex: July 1, 1967, to July 1, 1969. Washington, D.C.: U.S. Government Printing Office, 1970.

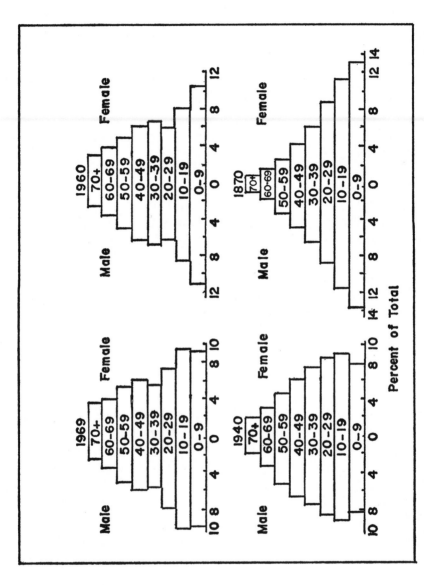

Figure 2–1. Distribution of the population by age and sex: 1870 to 1969. Source: reproduced from the United States Bureau of the Census, *Current Population Reports*, Series P 25, No. 411, March 19, 1970.

rather than to high fertility rates. If the United States ever reached a zero rate of population growth, the pattern would be that of a life table and would appear approximately as shown in Figure 2–2.

Birth rates are difficult to forecast. It is indeed possible that, at least for a limited period of time, another sharp increase in births such as occurred after World War II could appear. As the Census reports point out, however, "It would require a very substantial increase in births to reverse the long-term trend toward a more evenly distributed population by age."[2]

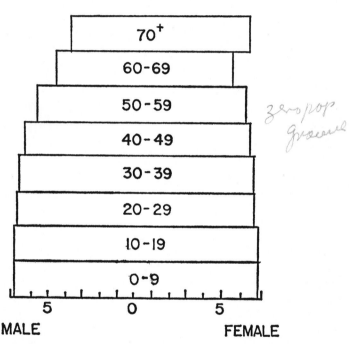

Figure 2–2. Age distribution of the population assuming a zero rate of population growth. (Based on the 1967 Life Table. Computed by A.J. Jaffe, Bureau of Applied Social Research, Columbia University.)

This maturing of the population is characteristic of advanced economic development where social, health, and medical forces operate more strongly than in newly-developed countries. In

2. *Ibid.*, p. 2.

an advanced economy birth rates tend to be relatively low, and death rates at the earlier ages decline.

If, as it appears, the age pattern of the population of the United States is approaching a rectangular form, there may be good reason to question some of the roles for various age groups that society has been assigning them in the recent past. Predominant among such assignments are more schooling for the young, and earlier retirement for more adults.

Yet it may take a very rich society indeed to support schooling until about age twenty and retirement at about age fifty, these two policies being dependent for the wherewithal on the productivity of those in their twenties, thirties, and forties. It must then be asked: what dependency ratio can society afford?[3] Perhaps a more crucial question is: what kind of dependency are we willing to pay for? The extreme inequality of treatment meted out to older members of the work force has been documented frequently. Some retire willingly and in prosperity; some are in a position to choose whether to work or to retire; many more retire unwillingly facing a future of low income as the penalty for not being permitted to work.

In 1870 few eyebrows were raised by the spectacle of the ten-year-old worker. Fewer still were raised because men worked until remitted by disability or death. In those days that was the way the work was accomplished. No argument is being made here that society does not order the work pattern better today, but the market forces by which the economy now operates are being played against a very different age pattern from that of a century ago. It may be necessary to take a new look at the labor force potential as the population pyramid vanishes.

---

3. For a discussion of possible dependency ratios see *Employment Aspects of the Economics of Aging*. Working Paper prepared for the Special Committee on the Aging, U.S. Senate (December 1969) by H.L. Sheppard, N. Sprague, and I. R. Withers.

Chapter 3

THE POSITION OF THE OLDER WORKER IN THE AMERICAN LABOR FORCE

RASHELLE G. AXELBANK

When unemployment figures make news, all workers begin to worry, but some will worry more than others, and with reason. Rising unemployment poses a real threat to older persons, a category variously defined as forty-five and over, fifty-five and over, or sixty-five and over.

The hardships of older jobseekers are often dramatized in terms of their long periods of unemployment. But their basic problem is employment. Economic developments have displaced them from old industries, lack of schooling has disqualified them from newer fields of work, and growth of private pension plans puts a premium on youth in hiring new employees.

Those who have been involved in counseling and placing older jobseekers know that there is age discrimination in hiring practices and are aware of the frustrations and humiliations that many older persons encounter. In fact, the complaints of older jobseekers brought the situation to public attention at least two decades ago and finally culminated in passage of the Age Discrimination in Employment Act which the President signed into law on December 15, 1967.

While some jobseekers begin to experience age discrimination as early as age forty-five, the difficulties for men become acute beginning at age fifty-five. The present dilemmas of older workers are largely an outgrowth of our economic past, a product of technological progress that has altered employment patterns, and a by-product of union gains in winning pensions. Economic progress embraces such developments as (a) the declining manpower needs in agriculture, mining, and railroading; proportion-

17

ately large numbers of employees in these industries were older workers; (b) vast changes in technology, creating new jobs for which older persons frequently lacked the required education; and (c) growth in private pension plans which have often gone hand-in-hand with upper age limits for newly hired men, a policy that curtails job opportunities for older persons.

A review of the past will clarify these developments. The data I present are drawn chiefly from a study prepared in the spring of 1968. This study centered on the problem of male workers.[1]

The overwhelming majority of older men in the labor force, generally more than 95 percent, do have jobs. Statistically, therefore, their problem does not appear to be great. But when we translate statistics into individuals, the figures assume a human meaning that must concern us deeply. In 1969, for example, perhaps one million men, aged forty-five and older, were unemployed at some time in the course of that year. That is not an insignificant number.

Changes in Industrial Employment Patterns

Between 1950 and 1960, employment of men in the nation rose almost 7 percent. This average figure tells us little, but the 7 percent comprised great expansion in some industries and sharp declines in others.

On the one hand, there were big increases in the following fields:

Education	+502,000
Public administration	+433,000
Finance, insurance, real estate	+327,000
Electrical machinery manufacture	+406,000
Aircraft parts manufacture	+318,000

At the other extreme were the sharp drops in other fields:

Agriculture	—2,509,000
Mining	— 286,000

---

1. Axelbank, Rashelle G.: The position of the older worker in the American labor force. *Employment of the Middle-Aged Worker.* New York, The National Council on the Aging, 1969, pp. 121–280.

Railroads — 429,000

Laundry, dry cleaning establishments — 58,000

The significant point about these changes is that the largest losses were in fields where large numbers of older men held jobs. These included agriculture, mining, railroads, and the self-employed.

Changes in employment occur at all times in our economy. But following World War II, the expansions and declines were of exceptional variety and magnitude. Although aware that employment is declining in their industry, older workers do not usually separate from their jobs until the jobs abandon them. Consequently older workers remained at their work as long as employers kept them. At the same time, the more mobile younger workers were absorbed into the newer expanding fields.

Two examples will illustrate this. In 1960, the median age of men in all industries was forty; in the fast-growing air-transportation industry it was thirty-five, but in the dwindling railroad operation the median was forty-seven.

The situation can be described in another way. Older workers were generally a disproportionately high percentage in declining industries, but a small proportion in expanding fields. Men aged forty-five and over held 46 percent of the jobs in retail apparel stores, where jobs were dropping, but only 30 percent in electrical machinery factories, where jobs were expanding.

Changes in Occupational Patterns

When the industry pattern is altered, changes in occupational patterns necessarily follow. The major changes in the 1947 to 1966 period were the growing proportion of workers in white collar fields, particularly in professional and technical jobs, and the declining percentages who were laborers and operatives. The great technological advances during these two decades created new areas of work requiring highly specialized personnel, and modified the job content of many traditional occupations.

Precisely as in industries, expanding occupations show a

younger-than-average work force, while contracting occupations show an older-than-average labor force in 1960. The median age of tailors and furriers was fifty-six years in 1960; that of airplane mechanics was thirty-eight years.

The impact of the foregoing changes on job opportunities for older men, once they lost their employment, can be predicted. When semiskilled and unskilled men past their mid-fifties looked for other work, many discovered that they were considered unqualified in the newer, expanding fields because they lacked the required education and work experience. Eventually, some settled for lower-paid work, or temporary employment or part-time jobs; still others, after prolonged unemployment, gave up the search and withdrew from the labor force.

This is not to imply that all older workers, once unemployed, fail to find good jobs. Unemployed persons, old or young, are a heterogeneous group, comprising the well-educated who offer the required skills and experience, as well as those who do not. However, tens of thousands among the older population, particularly men in various blue-collar and service occupations who had little schooling, feel they have been discarded, unjustly rejected by personnel staffs, simply because of age. They are supported in these views by investigators who find qualifications for many semiskilled and unskilled job openings to be excessive.[2]

Unemployment

The volume and rates of unemployment among men aged forty-five and older vary with the state of the economy, as among men of all ages. But in any given period, rates are usually lowest in the thirty-five to forty-four year group; thereafter they tend to rise with each successively higher age group. The year 1969 illustrates this point:

Age	Unemployment rate
45–54	1.5 percent
55–64	1.8 percent
65 and over	2.2 percent

2. See Jaffe, A.J.: Education and automation, *Demography* 3 (*No. 1*): 35–46, 1966.

These rates are deceptively low because they do not reflect a sizable volume of concealed unemployment. For example, these rates do not reflect the tens of thousands who drop out of the labor force because they believe they cannot find work; nor do the rates indicate the considerable volume of involuntary part-time employment. In 1969, some 233,000 men, aged fifty-five and over, worked part-time for lack of full-time jobs.

Men aged forty-five and over, jobless in any one week, averaged 332,000 in 1969. In the course of that year, perhaps one million men in this age group were without work at some time.

Long-Term Joblessness

The special problems of older workers are not reflected so much in their rate of unemployment as in the length of time they remain without work. They make up a disproportionately large percentage of the long-duration jobless. It is in this respect that their experience differs so widely from that of the younger population. It makes all the difference in the world to the morale of a jobseeker, and to the person who is doing the hiring, whether the applicant has lost his job a few weeks ago or half a year ago.

The statistics tell the story. Men aged forty-five and over accounted for only 24 percent of total male unemployment, but nearly 50 percent of male unemployment lasting twenty-seven weeks or longer in 1969.

Education and Unemployment

When advancing age is coupled with low educational levels, the difficulties in obtaining work are intensified. It is not surprising to find the highest jobless rates among the least educated of the older jobseekers. In one study, for example, men (aged 45 and over) with less than eight years of schooling showed an unemployment rate of 7 percent, compared with only 2.6 percent among high school graduates, and 1.1 percent among college-educated men.[3]

3. *The Older American Worker: Age Discrimination in Employment.* Report of the Secretary of Labor to the Congress Under Section 715 of the Civil Rights Act of 1964, Washington, U.S. Government Printing Office, June 1965, p. 12.

Average years of schooling of older men have been increasing, but they are below those of younger men. In March 1968, median years of schooling were between twelve and thirteen years for men aged eighteen through fifty-four, but less than eleven years for the fifty-five to sixty-four year group and only nine years for those sixty-five and older.

Dropouts from the Labor Force

An alarming development during the past two decades is the increasing number of older men who are withdrawing from the labor force. In 1968, there were 1,312,000 men, aged fifty-five to sixty-four, not in the labor force; this was 650,000 more than in 1947. Among the sixty-five-and-over group, 5,743,000 men were out of the labor force, an increase of more than three million from the 1947 figure.

Expressed in terms of labor force participation rates, the declines were as follows:

	Labor Force Participation Rates—Men	
Age	1947	1868
45–54	95.5	94.9
55–64	89.6	84.3
65 years and older	47.8	27.3

The decline in labor force participation is often cited as a reflection of our affluent society, which enables more and more men to retire early on adequate incomes. This may hold true for perhaps a third of the early retirees, but the story is quite different for the majority.

Why have more and more older men dropped out of the labor force? Some fifty thousand men between forty-five and sixty-four dropped out of the labor force in 1968 because they were discouraged about finding a job. Among 107,000 discouraged men aged sixty and over, the majority dropped out of the labor force in the belief that employers would not give them a job because of their age.[4]

---

4. Flaim, Paul O.: Persons not in the labor force: Who they are and why they don't work, *Monthly Labor Review, 92:* 3–14, July 1969.

The official reason given by early retirees for dropping out of the labor force is not always the real one. Ill health is the explanation most often cited, although inability to obtain a regular job is frequently the more basic cause. It is now recognized that humiliation and depression resulting from a long, unsuccessful job search may lead to symptoms of illness and disability; moreover, ill-health as a reason for not working is a more palatable explanation than is failure to find work.

Employment Income Versus Social Security Benefits

Most men under sixty-five, and many above that age, prefer employment to retirement for the simple reason that they need the larger incomes that jobs provide. Many early retirees return to work because they need the money.

It may be advantageous for men to obtain reduced benefits at age sixty-two or sixty-three or sixty-four, if they have lost hope of finding work, but it must be recognized that the size of the average benefit is only a fraction of income from employment.

Median earnings of employed men aged sixty to sixty-four, covered by the social security program, were $5,660 in 1967. Benefits in that year for retirees aged sixty-two to sixty-four years averaged below $1,000.

Early Retirees

Since the 1961 amendment which permitted men to retire at age sixty-two, with reduced benefits, more and more persons have chosen to apply for social security benefits before age sixty-five. Of the men who started receiving their old age pensions in 1968, 54 percent were under sixty-five and they received reduced amounts; the proportion receiving reduced benefits was still higher among the most recent awards.

Why are so many male heads of households choosing early retirement when it means smaller amounts not only for themselves but their wives as well? The answer appears to be that they believe they have no better alternative.

In terms of their employment histories, how do early retirees differ from men who defer retirement until age sixty-five? A recent analysis of men claiming retirement benefits in 1966 reveals that early retirees have less continuous employment and much lower lifetime earnings than those who retire at sixty-five. Among the early retirees, the percentage of men with low earnings (less than $2,400 in their last year with earnings) was almost three times higher than among retirees at sixty-five.[5]

In short, the majority of early retirees are the very men who can least afford any reductions in their old age benefits; they would be much better off if they were employed until age sixty-five and could retire at full benefits. It is difficult to avoid the conclusion that in a large proportion of cases, early retirement is an alternative to long-term unemployment or sporadic employment at low wages.

There is, to be sure, another aspect to early retirement. Perhaps one-third of the men who separate from jobs before sixty-five are those with adequate total incomes who can afford to do so and choose to do so.

Private Pensions and Age Discrimination

It is an irony that private pension plans, which mark an advance in economic security for millions of workers, have at the same time intensified age discrimination in the hiring process, curtailed job opportunities for many older men, and contributed to their longer unemployment.

The preference for younger workers in our society is recognized. Growth in private pension systems has reinforced this preference. Plants with established pension systems generally defend setting upper age limits for newly hired persons on the basis of the high cost of pension coverage for newly employed older workers. This cost-accounting approach by management in hiring practices is inconsistent with an enlightened labor market philosophy and calls for re-examination of private pension policies.

---

5. Bixby, Lenore E. and Rings, E. Eleanor: Work experience of men claiming retirement benefits, 1966, *Social Security Bulletin*, 32: 3–14, August, 1969.

Conclusion

Older jobless men are, by and large, victims of certain injurious forces that accompany industrial progress. When an older man comes to an employment office for assistance, it is important for the counselor to be aware that the applicant before him may have lost his foothold because of changes in industrial and occupational patterns in the economy—changes over which the applicant had no control and for which he was not prepared. The older applicant is likely to be discouraged, if not cynical. Understanding the circumstances that brought him to this state should enable counselors to work more sensitively and effectively with him. It is particularly important to keep in mind that early "retirement" may be a step toward poverty rather than a solution to the income problem.

TABLE 3-I
ESTIMATES, TOTAL POPULATION IN THE UNITED STATES
JULY 1, 1969
(in Thousands)

	Total	Men	Women
All Ages	203,216	99,771	103,445
45–54	12,192	5,900	6,292
50–54	10,987	5,298	5,690
55–59	9,904	4,737	5,168
60–64	8,309	3,895	4,415
65 and Over	19,470	8,295	11,175

Source: United States Department of Commerce, Bureau of the Census: *Current Population Report.* Series P-25, No. 428, August 19, 1969, Table 2.

TABLE 3-II
TOTAL MALE LABOR FORCE AND LABOR FORCE PARTICIPATION
RATES BY SELECTED AGE GROUPS
1947 and 1968

	Number (in Thousands)		Participation Rates	
	1947	1968	1947	1968
35–44 Years	9,603	11,122	98.0	97.2
45–54 Years	7,882	10,364	95.5	94.9
55–64 Years	5,650	7,030	89.6	84.3
65 Years and Over	2,376	2,154	47.8	27.3

Source: United States Department of Labor, Bureau of Labor Statistics: *Handbook of Labor Statistics.* Bulletin No. 1630, July 1969, Table 2, pp. 25–26.

Employment of the Middle-Aged

TABLE 3-III
MEN NOT IN THE LABOR FORCE, BY SELECTED AGE GROUPS
1947 and 1968
(in Thousands)

	1947	1968	Increase 1947 to 1968
35–44 Years	191	315	124
45–54 Years	369	552	183
55–64 Years	658	1,312	654
65 Years and Over	2,590	5,743	3,153

Source: United States Department of Labor, Bureau of Labor Statistics: *Handbook of Labor Statistics.* Bulletin No. 1630, July 1969, Table 6, p. 34.

TABLE 3-IV
UNEMPLOYED MEN, AGED FORTY-FIVE AND OLDER, BY
DURATION OF UNEMPLOYMENT
1969

		Number Unemployed in Average Week			
	Total	Less Than 5 Weeks	5–14 Weeks	15–26 Weeks	27 Weeks and Over
Men, All Ages	1,403,000	773,000	427,000	128,000	75,000
Men, 45 and Over	332,000	140,000	110,000	46,000	37,000
Men, 45 and Over as Percent of All Men	24	18	26	36	49

Source: United States Department of Labor, Bureau of Labor Statistics: *Employment and Earnings.* Vol. 16, No. 7, January 1970; based on data in Table A-13, p. 112.

TABLE 3-V
PATTERN OF UNEMPLOYMENT AMONG MEN AGED FORTY-FIVE
AND OLDER COMPARED WITH MEN OF ALL AGES
1969

	Number Unemployed in Average Week		Percent	
Duration of Unemployment	All Men	Aged 45 and Over	All Men	Aged 45 and Over
Total Unemployed	1,403,000	332,000	100	100
Less Than 5 Weeks	773,000	140,000	55	42
5–14 Weeks	427,000	110,000	31	33
15–26 Weeks	128,000	46,000	9	14
27 Weeks and Over	75,000	37,000	5	11

Source: United States Department of Labor, Bureau of Labor Statistics: *Employment and Earnings.* Vol. 16, No. 7, January 1970; based on data in Table A-13, p. 112.

TABLE 3-VI
PROPORTION OF MEN FORTY-FIVE YEARS AND OVER EMPLOYED
IN SELECTED INDUSTRIES AND OCCUPATIONS, 1960

	Percent change in Male Employment 1950 to 1960	Median Age	Percent Aged 45 and Over
All Industries	+ 6.9	40.6	39.4
Agriculture	−38.9	44.7	49.4
Railroads	−32.6	47.3	55.6
Retail Trade, Apparel	−18.1	42.6	45.9
Laundries and Cleaning Services	−17.9	42.5	44.0
Apparel Manufacturing	− 5.2	42.3	44.2
Electrical Machinery Manufacturing	+71.1	37.4	29.3
Aircraft Manufacturing	+141.6	38.7	29.6
Air Transportation	+89.9	35.6	19.0
Retail Trade, Autos, Accessories	+51.4	38.7	32.6
All Occupations	+ 6.9	40.6	39.4
Professional and Technical	+50.8	38.2	31.6
Airplane Mechanics	+60.3	37.9	24.4
Radio and TV Mechanics	+37.9	35.8	23.2
Operatives:			
Assemblers	+50.5	36.9	30.2
Attendants, Auto Service	+49.8	25.8	18.5
Fabricated Metals	+37.7	38.0	32.1
Electrical Machinery	+38.7	37.1	29.8
Paper	+17.9	35.7	27.4
Chemicals	+20.8	38.4	30.9
Farmers and Farm Managers	−43.1	49.2	60.7
Painters	− 7.5	45.2	50.4
Tailors and Furriers	−51.9	56.4	73.0
Elevator Operators	−21.4	52.2	65.7

Source: United States Department of Commerce, Bureau of the Census: *Census of Population 1960.* Vol. I, *Characteristics of the Population,* Part 1, United States Summary; based on data in Tables 202 (528–533), 204 (540–543), 211 (565–566), 212 (567–568).

II. THE OPTIONS: EMPLOYMENT VS. LEISURE

Chapter 4

LIFETIME TRADEOFFS
BETWEEN WORK AND PLAY

JUANITA M. KREPS

"In the world of common-sense experience the only close rival of money as a pervasive and awkward scarcity is time," Wilbert Moore noted half a decade ago. "Loyalty or affection, too, turns out to be a universal scarcity upon close examination . . ."[1] But ours is not a discipline that attends to questions of human emotions, and we are therefore allowed to ignore any vexing problems arising from too little (or too much) affection. We do profess expertise in matters of time and money and their allocation, however; the wonder is that we have spent so much time on money and so little on "the pervasive and awkward scarcity" of time itself.

The discussion following is concerned with the division of time between work and leisure and within that general issue with several specific questions. What do traditional theories of the allocation of time have to offer in explanation of the current distribution? What are the determinants of the forms of today's leisure? Finally, how do we explain the accrual of disproportionate quantities of free time to certain workers, and the failure of others to share in the growth of leisure?

I. The Rationale: Higher Wages, Less Leisure

Time has played an important role in economics—implicitly in classical theory and explicitly in neoclassical theory (espe-

Note: Reprinted from the *Industrial Relations Research Association Proceedings,* 1969, pp. 307–316.

1. Moore, Wilbert E.: *Man, Time and Society.* New York, Wiley, 1963, p. 4.

cially in the works of Marshall, Fisher, and Knight) and in Keynesian and post-Keynesian theory. But the emphasis has been on rates per unit of time, upon time patterns of consumption and production, and upon the implications of futurity.[2] On the relationship between income incentives (wage rates) and the quantity of labor offered, opinion has shifted through the centuries.[3] The mercantilists argued that the labor supply curve was negatively sloped, reasoning that men would work only long enough to maintain themselves ". . . in that mean condition to which they have become accustomed."[4] Adam Smith and J. B. Say took the opposite view, believing that a majority of workmen, when liberally rewarded, were likely to overwork and threaten their health. Malthus, as one would expect, held that the worker would toil only that number of days required for subsistence. The negative relationship was rejected by Marshall, but reaffirmed by Pigou.[5]

Contemporary views of the slope of the supply function are also diverse, although there seems to be some preference for the notion of a negatively-sloped curve, or at least one that is highly inelastic. G. F. Break argues that workers have fixed

2. For a recent discussion of the limitational role of time, see Spengler's analysis (Chap. IV) in Kreps, Juanita M., and Spengler, Joseph J.: The leisure component of economic growth. *Technology and the American Economy.* National Commission on Technology, Automation, and Economic Progress, Appendix, Vol. II, 1966. See also Shackle, G.L.S.: *Time in Economics.* Amsterdam, 1958.
3. See Joseph J. Spengler's review of the argument: Product-adding versus product-replacing innovations. *Kyklos,* X: 267–277, Fasc. 3, 1957.
4. Child, Josiah, quoted in Douglas, Paul H.: *The Theory of Wages.* New York, Kelley, 1934, p. 270.
5. See citations in Spengler, *op. cit.*: Smith, Adam: *An Inquiry into the Nature and Causes of the Wealth of Nations.* New York, Modern Library, 1937, pp. 81–86; Say, J.B.: *Traite d'economie politique.* Paris, 1841, Book II, Chap. 7, sec. 4; Malthus, T.R.: *An Essay on the Principles of Population.* London, 1826, pp. 368, 379, 424–425; Marshall, Alfred: *Principles of Economics.* London, Variorum edition, 1961, pp. 140–143, 526–529, 680–696, 720–721; Pigou, A.C.: *A Study in Public Finance.* London, 1929, pp. 83–84, and *The Economics of Stationary States.* London, 1935, pp. 163–164.

commitments, either with respect to the maintenance of certain goals, or to the observance of rigid work patterns. The pressures of these commitments force the worker to render a certain number of hours at any given wage rate, thus tending to make the supply curve inelastic; or else the commitments cause him to demand a certain level of income, which can be maintained with fewer hours of work as the wage rate rises.[6]

II. The Record: Higher Wages, More Leisure

Whatever the preference of the individual worker at any particular time, he has in fact gained both income and time free of work during the twentieth century. In annual hours, his free time has grown by about 1200, and in lifetime years, he has gained an additional nine that are free of work. The fact that workers have taken more and more free time, although each additional hour of free time was more expensive in terms of goods foregone,[7] would seem to conflict with the stereotype of the "thing-minded' American, who allegedly prefers a higher paycheck to a shorter workweek.

The conflict has often been dismissed with a reference to labor's belief that as long as there is unemployment, the work week is too long. Hence, working time is reduced because of the need to create additional jobs, and free time, like work, needs to be spread more evenly over the entire labor force, including the unemployed. Economists, proud of their sophisticated perception of the "lump-of-labor" theory, have been eager to debunk this trade union attempt to create jobs, but reluctant to deal analytically with the free time generated in the process of growth. An outstanding exception is Gary Beck-

---

6. Break, G.F.: Income taxes and incentives to work. *American Economic Review*, 47: September, 1947; also Duesenberry, James, *Income, Saving, and the Theory of Consumer Behavior*. Cambridge, Harvard, 1949.

7. See Long, Clarence D.: *The Labor Force Under Changing Income and Employment*. Princeton, N.J., Princeton University Press, 1958, Chap. 1, 2, and 13.

er's work, in which he gives nonworking time a value by including it in his concept of "full income."[8]

It seems perfectly reasonable for today's worker to take the position that the forty-hour week is not particularly onerous, but that his income is inadequate. For workers who have become accustomed to being at work (and whose colleagues typically work) the standard number of hours, the attraction of more time off probably has much less appeal than an increase in income. With wages rising in accord with productivity, the worker's true preference is illustrated by a perfectly inelastic demand for leisure (or supply of effort). Reduction below the "fair" or "customary" working time may have little support until some major policy decision changes the pattern of working time; even then, it may take some time for the shorter schedule to be generally accepted as the norm. But eventually workers will adjust to a six-hour day or a four-day week; it is easy to imagine, in fact, that after a period of time workers could come to view a standard workweek of thirty hours as quite appropriate, the forty-hour week being remembered in much the same way we now think of the ten-hour day.

III. The Games People Play

The distribution of lifetime between working years and leisure years depends primarily on the nation's stage of economic development, or more precisely, on the productivity of labor and hence the capacity to support nonworking periods of time. Labor force activity rates for men are highest in agricultural and lowest in industrialized countries, the average number of years of active and inactive life for men varying significantly.[9]

The fact that men have few inactive years in underdeveloped countries is attributable to rurality and low incomes, John Durand has noted; hence the appearance of nonagricultural indus-

---

8. Becker, Gary: A theory of the allocation of time. *Economic J, LXXV*: 493–517, Sept., 1965.

9. United Nations: *Sex and Age Patterns of Participation in Economic Activities.* New York, United Nations, 1962, Table 4.4. Figures are unweighted means.

	Average Net Years at Birth		Average Net Years at Age 15	
	Active Years	Inactive Years	Active Years	Inactive Years
Industrialized countries	42.2	22.8	45.3	9.2
Semi-industrialized countries	35.6	17.2	43.1	6.4
Agricultural countries	33.9	14.4	41.5	4.6

tries, the growth of cities, and increases in output per worker lead to a decline in male labor force activity at both ends of working life.[10] Irene Taeuber's study of Japanese demographic patterns reveals even more clearly than the European data a downward trend in activity rates for young and older men in the 1920 to 1940 period, despite Japan's wartime mobilization.[11] A more recent analysis, posing the question of whether as incomes rise people systematically change the distribution of their time between work and leisure, concludes that there is a significant negative correlation between income and the aggregate allocation of effort to income acquisition.[12] Of the variables other than income that explain the allocation of time, the most important is found to be the state of aggregate demand as indicated by the level of unemployment. The United States' high-income, high-unemployment position in recent years is thus compatible with a reduction in the amount of effort devoted to work.

High hourly wage rates and levels of unemployment may explain more than the decrease in time spent at work; they may also explain in part why leisure grows in one form rather than another, and in particular, why the free time is increasingly taken at the beginning and the end of worklife, rather

10. See Durand, John D.: Population structure as a factor in manpower and dependency problems of under-developed countries. *Population Bulletin of the United Nations*, New York, United Nations, 1965, No. 3, p. 6.
11. Taeuber, Irene B.: *The Population of Japan*. Princeton, Princeton University Press, 1958.
12. Winston, Gordon C.: An international comparison of income and hours of work. *Review of Economics and Statistics*, XLVIII: 28–39, Feb. 1966.

than during the workyear.[13] But there has been little specula-
tion and even less research on the forms in which leisure is
now emerging. As a result, we know very little about workers'
actual preferences as to the distribution of free time, although
the form in which leisure is made available surely conditions,
if not dictates, its utility.

Variations in leisure-time patterns occur even among nations
which are at roughly the same stage of economic development.
For illustration, we may take five countries: West Germany,
Sweden, Switzerland, the United Kingdom, and the United
States. Among these nations, the workweek varies from 38.5
hours to 45.5 hours; annual holidays range from two to four
weeks; public holidays may be as few as six and as many as
thirteen. As to the male's worklife, active years range from
39.7 to 45; inactive from 21.4 to 25.8; the proportion of life
that is active varies from 60.6 to 67.8 percent.

On a country-by-country basis, differences in working patterns are quickly apparent. Workers in Switzerland have a long
workweek but generous holiday provisions; participation rates
for males are high, and this applies to young and older men.
West Germany, too, has a long workweek offset by long vacations and frequent public holidays. But whereas German males
enter the labor force early, they also retire early. In the United
Kingdom, teenagers have exceptionally high activity rates and
old people relatively low rates. Vacation and public holiday
provisions are much less generous but the workweek is somewhat shorter than in Germany and Switzerland. In Sweden,
the amount of leisure and its allocation over the worklife differ
from the patterns in other countries. Swedish men have a short
workweek, frequent paid holidays, and extremely long vacations. They enter the labor force late, and retire late. Here,
the high activity rates for women, following the male pattern
in the timing of worklife, serves to spread nonworking time
somewhat more evenly between the sexes than is the case in
other countries.

---

13. The advantages of a gradual reduction in the workyear, and the rea-
    sons for the historical trend in this direction, were discussed by
    Clarence Long a decade ago. *Op. cit.*, pp. 24–25.

Workers in this country enjoy a shorter workweek than most countries in Western Europe, but fewer annual and public holidays. In the changing patterns of worklife, we resemble Sweden in one important respect: participation rates for men have declined and those for women have increased. Moreover, in these two countries men enter the labor force late. But there are important differences. In Sweden the high proportion of working women of all ages is partially offset by some reduction in working hours per week and by generous holiday arrangements. In the United States the increased labor force activity of women is being counterbalanced by the reduced participation of younger and older men.[14]

IV. A Lump-of-Leisure Theory

At any point in time, institutional arrangements largely dictate the terms of nonworking time, i.e. when it occurs, and who receives it. Compulsory retirement at age sixty-five is one example; the statutory forty-hour week, as well as negotiated vacation plans, helps to standardize the length of the workyear.

A major purpose of both the legislation providing for the eight-hour day and that establishing a retirement benefit scheme was to reduce the amount of labor offered by persons then at work (or viewed differently, to give to some workers additional free time), with the ultimate objective that within the new working rules everyone who wanted to work at going rates of pay could find jobs. Under pressure to create jobs during the depressed thirties, we thus reallocated time between work and leisure. One result of this reallocation was the acquisition of a large block of free time on the part of a particular group of workers, who were dropped from the active labor force altogether.

With the growing emphasis on retirement as a lifestage and some corollary improvement in retirement benefits, and with a possible movement toward early retirement, we may find our-

---

14. For sources of this comparative statement see Kreps, Juanita M.: *Lifetime Allocation of Work and Leisure.* Social Security Research Report, No. 22, 1968.

selves allocating a very large proportion of the leisure emerging in the process of economic growth to retirement. Lumps of leisure accruing at the beginning and again at the end of work-life could absorb most of our growth in nonworking time, in contrast to the earlier pattern in which leisure was translated into shorter workweeks.

Not only does the new leisure tend to be lumpy in its time dimension; that portion which accrues during worklife is also being spread quite unevenly over the work force with the result that certain groups of workers have failed to share in this component of growth. Harold Wilensky's analysis of the distribution of leisure[15] shows a disproportionate gain for workers in mining and manufacturing and (since 1940) in agriculture. By contrast, civil servants and the self-employed have gained little or none. Certain groups—white-collar workers, salesmen, clerks, proprietors, managers, officials, and most professions—tend to work full time year-round, while rural workers, women, nonwhite, young and old persons are employed part-time or intermittently.

The author concludes that higher-income recipients have probably lost leisure during the twentieth century. Among a sample of clerks, salesmen, craftsmen, foremen, small proprietors, semiprofessionals, technicians, managers, and some operatives, with incomes ranging from $5,000 to $13,000, about half worked forty-five hours or more weekly, and a sizeable minority worked sixty hours or more. One-third of the men earning $10,000 or over logged fifty-five hours or more per week. Within strata, differences in work schedules were also pronounced; lawyers and professors, for example, have much longer workweeks than engineers. Business executives average a workweek of fifty hours, excluding business entertaining at home, travel time to work, and business travel. Being self-employed, Jewish, or high-income tends to raise the propensity for long hours.

In summary, it appears that much of our leisure is coming

15. Wilensky, Harold L.: The uneven distribution of leisure. *Social Problems*, 9:32, 56, 1961–62.

to be concentrated temporally, occurring at the beginning and end of worklife; moreover, that the leisure available during worklife is being concentrated on certain groups, notably those workers who are in excess supply relative to the demand for their services. Mr. Wilensky is probably right in concluding that, given the bunching of leisure, the gains to some groups have been exaggerated, and furthermore that the quality of such fragmented leisure is far from ideal.

In our analysis of the supply of labor, we have perhaps been unduly concerned with variables which tell us little about the behavior of today's workers. For the low-skilled blue-collar worker in a declining industry, nonworking time (not counting unemployment) obviously grows as the demand for this type of labor declines, worker preference for income over leisure notwithstanding. The explanation for the growth in leisure lies altogether in the shortage of jobs relative to job seekers, and the consequent attempt to spread work. At the other extreme, professional, technical, and managerial workers are not gaining leisure, again because of the state of demand for their services. Shortages of labor in this sector result in a bidding up of wages and salaries, but not in the amount of labor offered in the short run, since most of these persons already have extremely heavy work schedules. The amount of leisure taken by the two groups of workers is thus independent of the price of labor, at least within a very broad range, the unskilled worker being willing to spend more hours at work at the going rate of pay, and the executive or professional not being able to spend any additional hours at work, even if offered higher pay.

In the long run, the promise of higher prices for skills and professional talent will of course induce more persons to make the necessary investment in education. But will it increase the supply fast enough to more than offset the rise in demand, and thus allow professional persons to have some increase in free time? Do business executives and members of the professions want free time? Or does the work orientation of men going into these areas preclude their acceptance of leisure in the amounts now available to blue-collar workers?

V. More or Less Puritan

Answers to these question are difficult in part because of the fuzziness of our definition of leisure.[16] For purposes of this discussion, the meaning usually conveyed—i.e. time not spent at work for pay—has been used. But there are serious short-comings of this concept, particularly when it applies to work-ers whose performance is largely dependent on high levels of education and training, and who must continue some measure of education as a condition of employment. For such persons, it is almost impossible to separate "work for pay" from the lei-sure-time pursuit of reading, attending professional meetings, etc. Compounding the problem is the perverse propensity of many of these men to prefer their work (with or without pay) to the world's more frivolous pastimes. Use of the term "non-working" time is of no help, since we have not defined work, and the whole question of involuntary unemployment continues to cloud the picture when leisure and nonworking time are used synonymously.

If a particular group of workers gain free time because of a decrease in the demand for their services, how do we view the additional nonworking time of the men who continue to be employed? When the free time is involuntary, it would seem to lie somewhere along the continuum of unemployment, under-employment, and leisure. On the other hand, if workers who can control their hours work far more than the minimum num-ber, even when their incomes are unaffected by the amount of time on the job, the extra time can hardly be thought of as work "for pay." Perhaps a concept of "discretionary work," defined as the difference between the amount of time a man actually works and the amount necessary to earn his current pay, would help to identify the extent of his preference for work over play, thereby removing the notion of a necessary pay incentive. Similarily, the man who finds it impossible to trans-late free time into work for pay may not be categorized as being at leisure; instead, he is in a sort of limbo in which he

16. For a review of the definitional problem, see Voss, Justin: The defi-nition of leisure. *J of Econ Issues*, 1:91–106, June, 1967.

must accept some involuntary or nondiscretionary free time. Important as new labels for the gray area between work and play may be for analytical purposes, the more critical issues arise from our failure to make explicit our preferences first, as between goods and free time and second, as to the preferred forms of any additional leisure. On the first issue, the vast range of our unmet needs[17] would seem to render untenable the acceptance of any involuntary leisure. On the second, a case can be made for diverting more and more of our time to education, investments in education being the corollary of our high current growth, and the *sine qua non* of future, even higher rates. Whether such an allocation of the leisure component of growth is actually preferred, particularly by the students themselves, has not been demonstrated, although it may be in time; they have already demonstrated on behalf of practically everything else.

---

17. See Lecht, Leonard: *The Dollar Cost of Our National Goals.* Washington, The National Planning Association, 1965.

Chapter 5

A NOTE ON INCOME VS. LEISURE
AS RELATED TO PRODUCTIVITY

LEON GREENBERG

Not so many years ago sociologists, economists, psychologists and others specializing in the problems of the older workers extolled retirement as the ultimate goal of working men. More recent literature, however, frequently takes a more negative view. Retirement is portrayed as possibly a misfortune and society is encouraged to find ways of keeping older workers employed rather than to find ways of encouraging their search for leisure. Stories are recounted of resistance to retirement and of disillusionment after retirement. In contrast, Professor Kreps' paper continues the positive view of retirement and other forms of leisure. This approach attempts to give the worker a reasonable and respectable choice between retirement and continuation of work. Further, the approach recognizes that leisure years depend on labor productivity.

Increased productivity, as measured by output per man-hour, can provide the basis for the options of increased income, or voluntary leisure, or both. Leisure can take many forms: a shorter workweek, longer vacations, more schooling and later entrance to the labor market, or earlier retirement.

After the turn of the century, in the years before forty hours became the "standard" workweek, a substantial part of the annual productivity gain was used to relieve the onerous burden of sixty or more hours of work per week. Since World War II most workers have preferred more goods and services to fewer hours of work—some chose longer hours in the form of moonlighting and overtime. At the same time, increased vacation time and a small reduction in the workweek took some share

42

of the productivity gain, especially among blue-collar workers. Retirement rates apparently increased also.

The statistics show that output per man-hour in the private economy doubled between 1947 and 1969. During that time, average real hourly compensation[1] of all persons working in the private economy also nearly doubled, rising by more than 90 percent. There was a drop of four hours, about 9 percent, in the average workweek, but this was also partly affected by workers' shifting among industries and by part-time work as well as by reduced weekly hours of work.

Sharp decreases in rates of participation in the labor force would seem to indicate significant increases in retirement rates in the postwar period. Participation rates—labor force as a percent of population—among older male workers were:[2]

	1947	1954	1969
45 to 54 years	95.5	96.5	94.6
55 to 64 years	89.6	88.7	83.4
55 to 59 years	n.a.	92.4	89.6
60 to 64 years	n.a.	84.3	75.8
65 years and over	47.8	40.5	27.2
65 to 69 years	n.a.	58.2	42.3
70 years and over	n.a.	28.7	18.0

What about the future? If productivity should rise at 3 percent per year—a rate which is consistent with the postwar experience—and if all the gains to be shared by workers were to be taken in the form of income, real average hourly compensation could double by 1990.[3] Per capita and family incomes which are, of course, affected by family size and number of family members working, could also double. If the latter

---

1. Wages, salaries, employer contributions to retirement, health and other plans, and other supplements adjusted for changes in the *Consumer Price Index.*

2. Source: Bureau of Labor Statistics and *Manpower Report of the President.* Washington, U.S. Department of Labor, March 1970, Table A–2.

3. It should be noted that higher productivity can lead to gains in real income either through increased wages or lower prices, or a combination of the two.

two can be assumed to show little or no change, then median per capita personal income could rise from $3,400 in 1968 to about $6,800 in 1990. Median annual family income could rise from $8,600 in 1968 to about $17,000 (in 1968 dollars) in 1990.

At the income levels indicated, there will be many families whose income will continue to be no more than modest, by American standards. Such families will continue to seek significant improvements in their levels of living. It, therefore, seems likely that workers will continue to choose higher income as one of the important benefits of productivity gains during the next twenty years.

Another influence on the choice of work or leisure is related to caretaking of the environment. Some of the future growth in productivity (and output) may have to be diverted to environmental improvement and maintenance, so that potential real incomes and leisure will have to bear some of the cost. If productivity growth can be advanced beyond its previous rate, it will provide an extra resource for improvements along several paths.

At the potential growth rates indicated, and within the constraints indicated, it appears likely that leisure will increase, perhaps at a higher rate than in the past twenty years. With the multiple choices available, it does not seem likely that any one of the forms of leisure will rise precipitously. The important thing is that workers will have greater economic freedom to choose between income and leisure, with retirement as one of the options.

Chapter 6

SOME OBSERVATIONS
ON EARLY RETIREMENT

RICHARD E. BARFIELD

T he following remarks are based primarily on material contained in the Survey Research Center monograph, *Early
Retirement*.[1] The discussion of a resurvey of the sample of automobile workers is based on data collection and analysis which
occurred after the publication of the monograph.[2]

Introduction to the Study

Early retirement, i.e. retirement before age sixty-five, has become an increasingly important phenomenon in the United
States. Slightly more than half the men who have applied for
social security benefits recently have taken the reduced benefits paid to early retirees. Although retirement before the conventional age of sixty-five was not especially uncommon in earlier years, such retirement was often associated with chronic
unemployment, obsolescence of job skills, and/or earnings
"that were characteristically low or that had dropped off substantially"[3] in the later years.

1. Barfield, Richard, and Morgan, James: *Early Retirement: The Decision and the Experience.* Ann Arbor, Institute for Social Research,
1969.
2. The report on this final part of the study of decision making on early
retirement will be available shortly from the Institute.
    The investigations summarized here were supported in part by grant
number 277 from the Social and Rehabilitation Service of the United
States Department of Health, Education, and Welfare, Washington,
D. C.
3. Epstein, Lenore A.: Early retirement and work-life experience. *Social
Security Bulletin, 29:3*, March, 1966.

More specifically, Social Security Administration earnings records show that

> . . . men who had elected to begin drawing social security benefits at age 62 were only half as likely as age-65 retirees to have earned as much as $4,800 (the maximum amount on which taxes were withheld and benefits were based) in any year before retirement

and that

> . . . early retirees "were almost four times as likely to have earned less than $2,400 in their best year since 1960."[4]

Another Social Security Administration study found, however, that "there seem to be more and more aged men who are well enough to work and who might get some kind of job if they were interested, but who prefer the leisure of retirement."[5] There have been substantial improvements in retirement-income-maintenance programs in recent years, i.e. improvements which were not available to the great majority of previous early retirees. Increases in OASDHI benefits have been significant, if not spectacular; perhaps more important has been the spread of private pension plans, many of which contain more or less comprehensive early retirement provisions. In particular, substantially liberalized early retirement benefits were negotiated during the fall of 1964 by the International Union-UAW (United Automobile, Aerospace and Agricultural Implement Workers of America) and various companies in the automobile and agricultural implement industries; under the agreement in force at the time of this study, an auto worker who satisfied certain maximum seniority and earnings requirements could retire as early as age sixty with a monthly pension of $400.

With this development as a major impetus, and with the belief that "a study of . . . the circumstances that favor or oppose early retirement is greatly needed in order to predict future trends and to assess their impact on the economy and

---

4. *Ibid.*, p. 7.
5. Epstein, Lenore A., and Murray, Janet H.: *The Aged Population of the United States.* Washington, U. S. Government Printing Office, 1967, p. 105.

the well-being of millions of people,"[6] the Institute for Social Research and the Michigan Health and Social Security Research Institute began, in the fall of 1965, a study of decision-making on early retirement. The primary focus has been on finding those factors which are important for the decision to retire voluntarily, that is, before one is compelled to retire by institutional arrangements or for health reasons. The factors investigated included attitudes toward employment including positive or negative evaluation of income earned and the kind of work done as well as the evaluation of conditions expected under retirement including satisfaction or dissatisfaction with expected retirement income and appreciation of or antipathy toward leisure. Supplementing this major part of the study was a survey of the situations and attitudes of the already-retired.

The study design provided for data collection from two sources: a representative sample of the national population and a random sample of workers around sixty years of age in the automobile industry. The auto workers formed a fairly homogeneous group which was eligible, as stated earlier, for a relatively attractive early retirement benefit program and which was involved at the time of initial contact in making a decision on early retirement. Yet homogeneity, i.e., blue-collar workers in a mass production industry who are entitled to similar retirement provisions, has obvious disadvantages; ability to generalize from findings obtained with a special group would be limited unless it were possible to place such findings in their proper broad frame. The representative sample of the national population provides heterogeneity of age, current income, occupation, and retirement provisions. Interviewing of the national sample was completed during 1966;[7] mail contact was initiated with the auto workers during the same year, and personal interviews were conducted in the summer of 1967. The auto workers who were interviewed in person in 1967 were

6. Study of decision making on early retirement: Unpublished study proposal of the Institute for Social Research, The University of Michigan, Ann Arbor, 1965.
7. A smaller, supplemental national survey was also taken during August-September 1968.

contacted again in the fourth quarter of 1969, primarily for two reasons: to ascertain whether the expressed retirement plans of those who were still at work in 1967 have been in fact carried out and to investigate satisfaction with retirement as the retiree moved further into the retirement period.

Summary of Findings

The effect on retirement planning of both situational and attitudinal variables was analyzed, the expectation being that both types of factors would loom as important in a decision to retire. However, the major finding of the study is that financial factors (primarily expected retirement income) are of principal importance in the retirement decision. Attitudinal variables had less influence, although usually operating in expected directions. Among both national and auto worker sample respondents, there was found a "threshold" level of retirement income which most people seemed to consider necessary to insure a reasonably adequate postretirement living standard. This level is about $4,000 per year. It is likely, though, that $4,000 is not an absolute figure, but one which reflected a consensus about the minimum income necessary to provide reasonably comfortable living after retirement. Thus, the "threshold" level may shift upward over time as living standards generally rise, and this upward movement should be all the faster if price level increases are not kept within reasonable bounds. Other economic aspects of retirement, such as number of dependents expected at retirement age, house equity at retirement age, and expected income from assets at retirement age, were also importantly related to retirement plans in both parts of the study.

Another situational variable, subjective evaluation of health, was found to be substantially correlated with planning early retirement in both parts of the study. Persons seeing their health as relatively declining were more likely than others to express plans for early retirement. Generally, other situational variables demonstrated little correlation with retirement plans.

In the national sample analysis, persons who looked forward to enjoying recreational activities such as hobbies, sports and travel were substantially more likely than others to opt for retirement before age sixty-five. Persons who expressed dissatisfaction with their jobs, either directly or by stating that they had thought of moving to a more promising or lucrative job, were more responsive to the idea of early retirement, as were those whose overall commitment to the "work ethic" seemed somewhat tenuous. For perhaps a variety of reasons, age was found to be negatively correlated with plans for early retirement; the younger the worker in the sample group, the more likely he was to opt for early retirement. Finally, perception of pressures toward retirement—from the employer, from the union, from colleagues—tended to induce a little accommodating behavior. But current income, occupation, education, whether the respondent supervised others as a regular part of his job, and the time required to travel to work all exhibited no systematic relationship with retirement plans.

The retirement plans of three subgroups of respondents—those having some college training, those fifty to fifty-nine years of age, and those fifty to fifty-nine years of age who were also members of labor unions—were analyzed with respect to the situational and attitudinal variables utilized in the whole sample analysis. It was found that the importance of the various predictors varied little in the three groups from the patterns observed for all respondents. For example, expected pension income and the other economic variables continued as the most important of factors for the retirement decision; the respondent's health remained salient in all subgroups, gaining in importance for the two older respondent groups; having hobbies to pursue after retirement and disliking one's job were, as before, associated with an increased likelihood of planning retirement before age sixty-five. An especially important finding, since it has been speculated that persons with more education would be more likely to be attached to their jobs and less satisfied with the idea of retirement than those with less education, was that respondents with college training seemed at least as receptive to the idea of early retirement as others and as strongly motivated by financial, health, and leisure-time considerations.

About 15 percent of national sample respondents expressed plans to retire after age seventy or to continue work as long as they were able, or said that they would *never* retire. The person who plans late retirement is likely to be self-employed and over fifty, earning less than $5,000 per year and expecting a relatively small retirement income. He enjoys his work and has developed few outside interests which he could pursue in the event of retirement.

It seems unlikely that the number of late retirers will become proportionally greater in the future. Self-employed small businessmen, who form a large part of this group, will probably not become relatively more numerous. As the general income level rises, and as social security and private pension improvements are forthcoming, there should be fewer persons with relatively low current and expected retirement incomes.

In the auto worker sample analysis, an investigation of the factors underlying actual retirement behavior as well as retirement planning was possible, since about a third of the workers had retired between the time of initial mail contact in 1966 and personal interviews in 1967. As implied above, retiring early and planning to retire early were found to depend most directly on available retirement income (from both social security, if the worker had reached age sixty-two, and private pension benefits). Further, persons who had difficulty keeping up with the job, and who were unable to do anything about it, were rather more likely either to have retired or to be planning to retire early. Some differences, however, were uncovered in the analysis. *Having retired early* was correlated fairly strongly with subjectively feeling that one's health had improved during recent years, while persons who saw their health as declining were most likely to express *plans to retire early*. This finding is entirely consistent with other findings that health, or at least *feelings* about health, may improve after retirement. For those auto workers who had retired when interviewed, no other factors—including satisfaction with job and with place of work, ease or difficulty in getting along with superiors, extent to which the work was repetitive, and ability to control the pace of the work—were found to be systematically related to having retired early. Among those workers who were still working when interviewed, several other factors seemed to be associated with planning retirement before age sixty-five: the factors included such issues as having talked about "the question of when to retire" with people outside the immediate family, thinking that most younger people feel that older workers should retire to provide job openings, preferring less work than one is now doing or not preferring more work, and planning to spend time on leisure activities after retirement. We concluded that the auto worker tended to make prompt use of the new early retirement provision if his available retirement income was of a size to assure reasonably comfortable living; he remained at work, perhaps only so long as was necessary to raise his prospective income, if this were not so.

While the major focus of the study was on the decision to retire or to remain at work, sufficient information was obtained from retired individuals, in both the national and the auto worker samples, to arrive at some conclusions about the financial status of retired persons and to ascertain some of the factors leading to satisfaction or dissatisfaction with life after retirement. Since the findings referring to financial status are based on a national survey in 1966, they are perhaps somewhat dated now but may still be suggestive of the current situation.

It was found, as expected, that the income of retired people generally is substantially lower than that of the nonretired. Nevertheless, the data did indicate a substantial improvement in the income of the retired during the several years preceeding 1966:

In 1957 the median income of the retired was 37 percent of the overall median; in 1959 it was 42 percent; in 1965, 47 percent.

In 1959 close to one-half of all retired families had a family income of less than $2,000, while in 1966 only one-third of the retired fell in this income bracket (figures are in 1966 dollars).

The median income of families where the family head was retired was $2,400 in 1959 as against $3,100 in 1966 (figures are in 1966 dollars).

These overall figures do not take into account substantial income differences among the retired. Younger retirees have much higher current incomes than older retirees. For example, the median income of retirees under sixty years of age was $3,800 in 1965 as contrasted with a median of $2,500 for those age seventy or older; 20 percent of the former group had incomes of less than $2,000, while 39 percent of the latter had such incomes. The younger retired are also the better educated. Since education is highly correlated with earned income, it was inferred that the observed income differences are associated with similar differences in preretirement incomes. This inference is supported by several findings:

> The proportions of older and younger retirees who received income from postretirement jobs during 1965 were about the same.

> The retiree's subjective evaluation of his living standard now compared with that enjoyed before retirement varied only slightly across *age* groups.

> Subjective evaluations of differences between current and preretirement incomes were similar for older and younger retirees.

Perhaps the most interesting findings about the retired relate to differences between respondents who retired as planned (41 percent of all retirees) and those who were forced to retire unexpectedly, most often because of health, and at times because of job loss. Incomes were higher for those who retired as planned; their median income was $4,000 as opposed to $2,800 for the unexpected retirees. Eighty percent of the expected retirees had savings available when they retired; 62 percent of the unplanned retirees had savings. Presumably because of their generally more favorable economic position, those who retired as planned were less likely to have consumed part of their savings since retirement.

Turning to a subjective measure of economic welfare, 73 percent of the expected retirees claimed to be enjoying a living standard which was as good as or better than that to which they were accustomed before retiring; only 52 percent of the unexpected retirees were in this position. Finally, the major difference between these groups is that nearly 70 percent of those who retired as planned felt favorably about their retirement when they ceased working, while less than 20 percent of the unexpected retirees expressed similar feelings. Incidentally, it is worth noting that these differences exist whether the person retired before, at, or after age sixty-five.

It appears that retired persons are reasonably well satisfied with their lot. In both parts of our study about three-fourths of retired respondents reported being "satisfied" or "very satisfied" with their life since retirement. Among national sample respondents, satisfaction with retirement was substantially correlated with having an annual retirement income of $4,000 or more and with viewing one's present living standard as better than or the same as that enjoyed before retirement. Retirees who had retired as planned, rather than unexpectedly, were more likely to be enjoying retirement, as were those who had not had health problems serious enough to interfere with their preretirement work. Finally, relatively younger retirees, and those who had retired between ages sixty and sixty-five, were somewhat more satisfied with retirement than others.

Among auto worker respondents, several situational factors were conspicuously associated with retirement satisfaction; these included owning one's home mortgage-free, having over $10,000 in assets, being married, and having a substantial pension income. After the effects of the important situational variables were accounted for, the following other factors were found to be positively correlated with satisfaction:

having retired as planned, rather than unexpectedly

being in relatively good health

having attended at least one retirement information meeting (sponsored by the union and/or the company of employment)

participating in leisure activities.

By far the most important reason for auto worker dissatisfaction with retirement seemed to be serious health problems, either for the respondent himself or for other family members.

The Resurvey of the Auto Worker Sample

The auto workers, who were interviewed in 1967, were resurveyed during the fourth quarter of last year; the interviewers were able to reestablish contact with nearly 85 percent of those talked with earlier. While analysis of these data is currently in process, some comments on realization of previously expressed retirement plans and on continuing satisfaction with retirement are now possible.

The auto workers surveyed in 1967 fall into three nearly equal groups: the retired, those still at work but planning to retire before age sixty-five, and those planning to continue work until age sixty-five or later. The new data reveal that slightly over two-thirds of the sample have retired; thus, the ratio of persons at work to persons retired has been reversed almost in the period since the initial personal interviews. This gross evidence that early retirement plans have been substantially realized is supported by the further finding that there is a substantial correspondence between the expected retirement age as stated in 1967 and the actual retirement age as reported by those who have retired since that time. There are those, especially among the relatively small group still at work, whose retirement plans have apparently changed;[8] health, financial, and family-related factors are most often cited as reasons for having changed one's plans.

About one-quarter of auto workers who were still at work toward the end of last year still report plans to retire early. Here, a combination of attitudes and expectations similar to those noted in the earlier discussion seems to be operating: compared with persons who say they will continue to work, those who plan early retirement are more likely to look forward to a favorable financial situation after retirement and to

---

8. When queried directly, about one-quarter of nonretired respondents claimed to have changed their retirement plans; this fraction seems consistent with preliminary, more objectives measures of change in plans.

report that they are eligible for the negotiated early retirement benefit; they are less likely to say they are satisfied with their job; they are less likely to be able to control the pace of their work and more likely to find it hard to keep up with the work. Further, the planned early retirers are more likely to report that their health has declined during recent years, that they have lost more than ten workdays because of illness during the previous year, and that they suffer from a work-limiting disability. There are some differences from what was observed before. For example, those planning early retirement seem hardly more likely to have various postretirement activities which they wish to pursue after retirement than do the other auto workers. But it does seem that many of the factors whose importance for the retirement decision was inferred before are still significant for auto workers.

Satisfaction with retirement continues at a high level among auto workers. And, to the extent that change has occurred in feelings about life since retirement, it has more often than not been in the direction of increased satisfaction; currently 67 percent of retired auto workers report being satisfied with re-tirement, 19 percent report mixed feelings, and 12 percent report dissatisfaction. It is true, though, that some of those who reported feeling satisfied wih retirement in 1967 now seem somewhat less sanguine about things; for example, 40 percent of those who said they were "very satisfied" in 1967 now re-port feeling satisfied or ambivalent about retirement. On the other hand, retirees are likely to say that they are enjoying retirement more rather than less as they move farther into the retirement period; and this is especially true among those who reported being satisfied in the 1967 survey. Further evi-dence of general satisfaction with retirement may be inferred from the following: an overwhelming majority (89 percent) of all retirees believe that their decision to retire when they did was the right decision; about three-quarters of retirees would advise others to retire at the same age as they did; most re-tirees now report finding retirement "about" or "exactly" as expected. It appears that those retirees who did not share in the general feeling of satisfaction often suffered from health deficiencies which precluded their full enjoyment of the experience.

It is important to realize that the auto worker retirees constitute a retirement elite; several questions on their postretirement financial situation serve to emphasize this point. Over three-fourths of the retirees have not found it necessary to dip into their savings since retirement; 20 percent have in fact *increased* savings. About two-thirds claim to be spending as much as or more than before retirement. Over three-fourths view their living standard as being at least as high as that enjoyed before retirement; and of those who see some deterioration in standard of living, about one-half still believe they have enough to live comfortably. Inflation is seen as somewhat troublesome, but less than one-fifth view it as having had a substantial effect on their living standard. Probably deriving from their favorable financial situation is the further finding that relatively few auto worker retirees have increased the amount of home-based productive activity since retirement, and only 17 percent have undertaken any work for money.

Feelings about health continue in the pattern observed from the 1967 data. Of those respondents still on the job who report a change in health during the last two years, the great majority say their health is worse now. But for retirees whose health has changed, about as many claim to be feeling better as claim to be feeling worse now; further, over one-third of all retirees believe their health has improved since retirement, as opposed to about 16 percent who see it as having deteriorated. Among auto workers as for other groups in which careful studies have been carried out, retirement seems definitely associated with the maintenance of satisfactory health or at least health *feelings*.

Finally, the auto workers' answers to a series of questions referring to postretirement activities strongly imply that this group of retirees is *not* "disengaging from life:"

32 percent report spending more time on volunteer work now

48 percent report spending more time on leisure activities such as hobbies, crafts, and sports now

53 percent claim to be visiting relatives and friends more often now

51 percent claim to be more interested now in keeping up with world events.

While such answers may be subject to some reporting error, the consistency of the several responses certainly leads one to believe that auto worker retirees are maintaining interest in and interaction with the world around them.

Conclusions

The study of retirement decision-making implies that, even allowing for some wishful thinking, the proportion of people retiring early will increase. Evidence from the national sample part leads one to believe that, during the last five or six years, there has been some tendency for early retirement *planning* to become more common. The following table summarizes the findings from three surveys in which questions inquiring about planned retirement age were included:

| Age | Proportion Who Plan to Retire Before They Are Age 65 | | |
	1963 Survey (%)	1966 Survey (%)	1968 Survey (%)
35–44	25	43	34
45–54	23	33	35
55–64	21	22	26

Some differences in the questions asked of the respondents and in what preceded them may have had some effect on the responses. Yet it seems clear, first, that younger people are rather more likely than older people to think of retiring early and, second, that recent developments have influenced retirement plans. To be sure, the apparent decline from 1966 to 1968 in the proportion planning early retirement among younger persons (age 35 to 44) casts some doubt on the validity of a trend toward early retirement, but it should be noted that the overall proportion planning to retire before age sixty-five was essentially identical in both years (34 percent in 1966 and 33 percent in 1968). Thus, the approximately 10 percentage point increase in planned early retirement which was observed between 1963 and 1966 was maintained from 1963 to 1968.

It is likely, then, that more and more early retirees will be people who planned for early retirement and are financially prepared for it. The result is likely to be an increasing discrepancy among the retired between those who retired as they had planned to and those who retired unexpectedly, often without planning and hence in most cases with inadequate retirement incomes. The discrepancies will probably be accentuated by the growth of private pension plans covering only some workers and (in some cases) not even all the workers in any particular company or industry. One of the authors of *Early Retirement* has offered the following as a suggestion for alleviating this dichotomization of future retirees:

> The implications of this for policy with respect to OASDHI are that perhaps the most important revision might be the introduction of a provision by which workers would make voluntary supplemental contributions to the system and thereby raise their retirement benefits. In this way workers in jobs without supplemental private pensions could provide similar supplemental benefits through the Social Security System efficiently. There would be some competition with private pension and annuity plans, but for the most part only with the individual, not the group, plans; and the proposed scheme would be a great deal more efficient than individual private schemes.
>
> Earlier retirement could also be handled this way, by allowing additional worker contributions to build a fund similar to the supplemental early retirement benefits the auto workers now have. Indeed, it could be left flexible whether the worker would use his extra payments to provide earlier retirement, or to provide higher benefits upon regular retirement.[9]

The vigorous response of auto workers to the improved early retirement package (three-fourths either having retired or planning to retire early) would seem to imply that an increase

---

9. Letter from James N. Morgan to Harrison A. Williams. In Special Committee on Aging, United States Senate: *Long-Range Program and Research Needs in Aging and Related Fields.* Washington, Government Printing Office, 1968, p. 262.

in pension benefits will lead to a significant increase in early retirees. It is important to realize, however, that the increase in negotiated pension benefits provided by the 1964 agreement was indeed a substantial one; and it seems quite likely that a gradual improvement in pension levels, either through the social security mechanism or via private pensions, will not have such a dramatic impact on the number of early retirees. Given the "threshold" phenomenon discussed earlier it is probable that a continuation of the present pace of OASDHI improvements and private pension expansion will have a notable effect on early retirement only after we are well into the 1970s. A speeding up of the early retirement process, beyond that which is apparently occurring now, would seem to require either large increases generally in retirement-income-maintenance schemes or a selective distribution of available funds among particular groups of workers.

A finding which bears reiteration is that retirement can be a genuinely satisfying time of life for many, if not most, people. The design of the study renders this judgment somewhat tentative for national sample respondents, but a reading of the auto worker responses leads one to believe that it certainly can be true for this type of mass-production-industry worker. And this is important to know because some observers, noting the considerable increase in leisure time which future productivity increases probably will make possible, have questioned whether a choice to appropriate a large part of this increase to the retirement years would be wise. Their arguments are often persuasive. But the expressions of joy in the freedom of retirement on the part of a large majority of auto workers are also persuasive and should perhaps be considered when we arrange our priorities. Further investigation into the satisfaction afforded by retirement would seem to be worthwhile before a decision on the allocation of leisure time is made.

III. UNEMPLOYMENT:
SURVEYS OF THE MIDDLE-AGED

Chapter 7

WITHDRAWAL FROM THE LABOR FORCE
BY MIDDLE-AGED MEN, 1966–1967

HERBERT S. PARNES AND JACK A. MEYER*

T his report presents an intensive analysis of the characteristics of ninety-eight middle-aged men who withdrew from the labor force between the summer of 1966 and the summer of 1967.[1] Although the sample is very small, it is representative of approximately one-fourth of a million men in the United States population between the ages of forty-five and fifty-nine whose labor market status changed in that way between the two dates. By a rather microscopic examination of the characteristics of these men in relation to the characteristics of all men of the same ages who were in the labor force in the summer of 1966, we hope to shed additional light on the factors affecting the labor force participation of this age group of men and, particularly, to be able to make some generalizations about the *process* of labor force withdrawal.

---

* This report was prepared as part of a larger study being conducted by The Ohio State University, Center for Human Resource Research under contract with the Manpower Administration, United States Department of Labor. Interpretations or viewpoints contained in this report are solely those of the authors and do not necessarily reflect the official position or policy of the Department of Labor.

1. The phrase "withdrawal from the labor force" refers solely to the fact that a group of respondents who were in the labor force in the summer of 1966 were not in the labor force in the summer of 1967. We do not know what fraction of this group may have changed labor force status more than once during the intervening period. Furthermore, it cannot be assumed that the change in labor force status of the men under consideration is a permanent one.

I. BACKGROUND

During the past decade and a half there has been a perceptible decline in the labor force participation rate of both middle-aged and older men who have not yet reached the conventional retirement age of sixty-five. While the drop has been most pronounced in the fifty-five to sixty-four year age category, it has also occurred to a lesser extent among those forty-five to fifty-four. Between 1955 and 1969 the labor force participation rate of the older of these two groups declined by 4.5 percentage points (from 87.9% to 83.4%) while that of the younger category dropped almost two points (from 96.5 to 94.6%). The decreases were somewhat sharper among black men[2] than among white, especially in the group forty-five to fifty-four years of age. In that age group the drop in participation rate for the blacks was three times as great as for whites (4.7 versus 1.6 percentage points); among men fifty-five to sixty-four years old the intercolor difference was substantially smaller (5.2 versus 4.5 percentage points). As a consequence of these trends, the intercolor differential in participation rates of men forty-five to sixty-four years of age which had developed in the post-World War II period and which was 3.2 percentage points in favor of white men in 1955, had grown by 1969 to 5.5 percentage points.

For purposes of human resource policy, it is important that the reasons for these trends be clearly understood. For example, to the extent that the overall downward trend in labor force participation among men in this age category is merely a reflection of increasing levels of nonlabor income and the desire for more and earlier leisure, the situation is essentially a healthy one. On the other hand, if it reflects an increasing incidence of health problems, an accelerated rate of skill obsolescence, or increased age discrimination in the labor market so that labor force withdrawals are to a considerable degree involuntary, remedial manpower policies may be called for. Sim-

---

2. The figures for black men cited in this paragraph are actually the official Labor Department data for "Negroes and other races." All data in this paragraph are from *Manpower Report of the President, 1970.* Washington, U. S. Government Printing Office, 1970.

ilarly, the intercolor difference in labor force participation suggests one set of policies if it results from a health differential between whites and blacks, another if it is attributable to differences in education and training, a third if it is explainable primarily in terms of discrimination against blacks, and still something else if it is due largely to differences between the two groups in attitudes toward work.

A considerable amount of attention has been directed in recent years to the factors affecting labor force participation of this as well as other groups in the population. Most of these studies have been based on either 1960 Census data or on the Current Population Survey. In the case of Census data, the one-in-a-thousand sample from the 1960 Census has been used to investigate relationships between a variety of economic and social characteristics of individuals and their labor force participation. Analyses have also been based on data for cities or Standard Metropolitan Statistical Areas; in these cases the influence of demographic and economic characteristics of communities on local labor force participation rates has been examined. Finally, since January 1967 the Current Population Survey has included questions on the characteristics and the work intentions of persons not in the labor force. On the basis of all these studies a number of factors have been identified that appear to be important in determining the labor force status of middle-aged and older men. In brief, other things being equal, participation in the labor force tends to be associated with being married, being in good health, being well-educated, having high potential earnings, and not having access to sufficient nonlabor income for support.[3]

II. NATURE OF DATA

The present study analyzes the labor force participation of middle-aged men on the basis of a rather unique set of data.

3. For a review of the literature, see Parnes, Herbert S.: Labor force and labor markets. In *A Review of Industrial Relations Research*, Madison, Wisconsin, Industrial Relations Research Association, 1970, Vol. I pp. 1–33.

In mid-1966, interviews were conducted with a probability sample of the civilian noninstitutional population of men who were then between forty-five and fifty-nine years of age.[4] Questions identical to those used in the Current Population Survey were the basis for establishing the labor force and employment status of the men in the calendar week prior to the survey. In addition, questions were asked relating to a large number of economic, social, and psychological characteristics of the men including their previous work experience, their health, their financial status, the characteristics of their families, and their attitudes toward work in general and toward their jobs.

As the second stage in a planned five-year study of this cohort, the same sample was reinterviewed approximately twelve months later.[5] Using the calendar week preceding the date of interview in each year as the point of reference, 1.8 percent of the men reinterviewed in 1967 had withdrawn from the labor force during the course of the year, while 1.1 percent had moved in the opposite direction.[6] These percentages represent approximately 257 thousand and 154 thousand men, respectively. The present report focuses on the former group,

---

4. For a description of the sampling procedure and the content of the interview schedule, see Parnes, Herbert S., Fleisher, Belton M., Miljus, Robert C., Spitz, Ruth S. et al.: *The Pre-Retirement Years: A Longitudinal Study of the Labor Market Experience of the Cohort of Men 45-59 Years of Age.* Columbus, Ohio State University, Center for Human Resource Research, 1968, Vol. I.

5. See Parnes, Herbert S., Egge, Karl, Kohen, Andrew I., and Schmidt, Ronald M.: *The Pre-Retirement Years: A Longitudinal Study of the Labor Market Experience of Men.* Columbus, Ohio State University, Center for Human Resource Research, 1970, Vol. II.

6. There is reason to suspect that the extent of withdrawal from the labor force during a twelve-month period among men in this age category is understated by these data. Attrition in the sample between the survey dates was 5.8 percent of those initially interviewed in 1966, of which 1.2 percent resulted from known deaths, 2.5 percent from refusals to be reinterviewed, and 2.1 percent from inability to be located. It seems plausible that the last mentioned group includes a disproportionately high number of men who moved out of the labor force.

which is represented by ninety-eight sample cases, fifty-six white and forty-two black men.[7]

Thus, the ninety-eight sample cases on which this analysis rests represent middle-aged men observed in the process of withdrawing from the labor force. The longitudinal nature of the study allows us to describe characteristics of the group that were ascertained *before* their withdrawal. This has the substantial advantage of eliminating or at least considerably reducing the ambiguity that frequently exists in associations among variables in the cross section. For example, where a relationship is observed in cross-sectional data between labor force status and men's self-rating of their health, it is never absolutely clear to what extent this occurs because poor health has forced men out of the labor force and to what extent it reflects the attempt of those who have left the labor force for other reasons to rationalize their behavior. The advantage of

7. The large number of black men in this sample relative to white is primarily attributable to the fact that the sample design deliberately overrepresented blacks in a three-to-one ratio in order to permit statistically reliable estimates for them. In addition, black men evidenced a somewhat higher rate of withdrawal from the labor force than white men. Between the two survey dates 3.0 percent of the black men as compared with 1.7 percent of the white men had moved out of the labor force. Because of the different sampling ratios of the blacks and whites, and because the analysis in this study is based upon unweighted observations, the two color groups are treated separately throughout the analysis.

While the distributions of labor force dropouts are based on unweighted sample observations, the distributions of all men in the labor force in 1966, with whom the dropouts are compared in most of the tables, are based upon "blown-up" population estimates. Since sampling ratios are fairly uniform *within* each color group, no substantial bias can be introduced by this procedure. The data for the labor force dropouts and for all those in the labor force in 1966 differ in yet another respect. For all those in the labor force in 1966, the term "blacks" is used to refer to the category described in official government data as "Negroes and other races." In the sample of dropouts, however, the "black" category includes only Negroes. There was one sample case of a labor force withdrawal by a man falling in the category of "other races," but this was eliminated from the data.

longitudinal data is even clearer when attitudinal variables are related to labor force status.

Despite these advantages, our data suffer from several serious limitations, the chief of which is the small numbers involved. A much more useful analysis of this kind will be possible at the conclusion of our five-year study of the cohort, by which time a considerably larger proportion of the sample will have left the labor force. Another limitation of the data is that they emerge from a research project that was not specifically designed for the case-study approach undertaken here. As a consequence they are frequently not as detailed as we should have liked. There have been numerous instances as we have scrutinized individual cases in which we should have very much liked to be able to ask additional probing questions. Nevertheless, despite these limitations, the data do provide valuable insights into the process of withdrawal from the labor force.

The following section seeks to identify the factors responsible for labor market withdrawal by comparing the characteristics of the labor force dropouts with those of all men who were in the labor force in 1966. In Section IV we attempt to assess the prospect for reentry to the labor force. Section V contains a series of individual profiles of the dropouts, each being a prototype of a different path of withdrawal. The final section summarizes the findings.

III. THE CORRELATES OF LABOR FORCE WITHDRAWAL

Demographic and Occupational Characteristics

As Table 7-I indicates, the labor force dropouts tend to be more heavily concentrated in the oldest of the three five-year age categories covered by the sample, although it should be emphasized that as many as three-fifths were under fifty-five years of age in 1966. The relationships that other studies have found between marital status, education, and occupation on the one hand and labor force participation on the other are also clearly evident in these data. Among whites (although not in the case of blacks) the labor force dropouts are less likely

TABLE 7-I

COMPARISON OF LABOR FORCE DROPOUTS 1966–1967, WITH ALL MEN
IN THE LABOR FORCE, 1966, BY COLOR: SELECTED DEMOGRAPHIC
AND OCCUPATIONAL CHARACTERISTICS

	Proportion of Respondents with Indicated Characteristic	
Characteristic	Labor Force Dropouts, 1966–1967	All Men in Labor Force, 1966
55–59 Years Old in 1966		
Whites	41	28
Blacks	40	27
Married in 1966		
Whites	78	91
Blacks	83	83
Completed Less Than 12 Years of School		
Whites	62	56
Blacks	96	82
Completed 13 or More Years of School		
Whites	20	19
Blacks	2	7
White-Collar Workers, 1966		
Whites	23	40
Blacks	7	15
Blue-Collar or Service Workers, 1966		
Whites	53	51
Blacks	72	74
Farm Workers, 1966		
Whites	23	9
Blacks	21	11
Self-Employed, 1966		
Whites	33	20
Blacks	16	12

than all men in the labor force in 1966 to be married. In the case of both color groups, they are less likely to have achieved a high school diploma and, at least in the case of the blacks, are also less likely to have had any college training. The same relationship is apparent in the occupational data. White-collar workers are substantially underrepresented among the dropouts of both color groups and farm workers are substantially over-represented. By class of worker, the dropouts are more likely than all those in the labor force in 1966 to have been self-employed.

Health

Among men younger than the conventional age of retirement, one expects poor health to be a major explanation for non-labor-force status. It is interesting to inquire to what extent

measures of health obtained in the 1966 interview serve as predictors of withdrawal from the labor force between 1966 and
1967. Two health measures were used. Respondents were
asked: "Would you rate your health, compared to other men
of about your age, as excellent, good, fair, or poor?" They were
also asked whether their health or physical condition kept them
from working, or limited the kind or amount of work they could
do. Since all the men under consideration here were actually
in the labor force in 1966, none could have legitimately responded that he was prevented entirely from working.

The very substantial role of poor health in explaining withdrawals from the labor force of men in this age category is indicated by the data in Table 7-II. While fewer than one in
twenty of all of the men in the labor force in 1966 reported
that their health was "poor," the proportion was as high as

TABLE 7-II

COMPARISON OF LABOR FORCE DROPOUTS, 1966–1967, WITH ALL MEN
IN THE LABOR FORCE, 1966, BY COLOR: SELECTED
HEALTH CHARACTERISTICS

Characteristic	Proportion of Respondents with Indicated Characteristic	
	Labor Force Dropouts, 1966–1967	All Men in Labor Force, 1966
Reported "Excellent" or "Good" Health in 1966*		
Whites	43	79
Blacks	31	72
Reported "Poor" Health in 1966*		
Whites	30	3
Blacks	31	5
Reported Health Problem Affecting Work, 1966†		
Whites	61	22
Blacks	62	21
Reported Worsening of Health, 1966–1967‡		
Whites	64	10
Blacks	68	14
Reported Health Problem Affecting Work, 1967†		
Whites	64	26
Blacks	71	28

* "Would you rate your health, compared with other men of about your age, as excellent, good, fair or poor?"
† "Does your health or physical condition (a) keep you from working? (b) limit the kind of work you can do? (c) limit the amount of work you can do?"
‡ "Would you say your health or physical condition is better, about the same, or worse than a year ago?"

three out of ten among those who withdrew from the labor force during the ensuing twelve months. Similarly, whereas only one-fifth of all men claimed to have had health problems that in some way limited their work in 1966, such limitations were reported by three-fifths of those who were to drop out of the labor force. Based upon responses in the 1967 interview, approximately one-tenth of all those in the labor force in 1966 reported a worsening of health between the two survey dates, but this proportion was two-thirds in the case of those who had dropped out of the labor force. By the 1967 interview date, somewhat over one-fourth of the 1966 labor force members had health problems that limited their work ability in one way or another, while this was true of almost two-thirds of those who had withdrawn from the labor force—64 percent of the whites and 71 percent of the blacks.

The work-limiting health problems reported by the labor force dropouts were of rather long standing, and even more so for the blacks than for the whites. The average duration of such problems was about eight years for the former and twelve years for the latter. Only 10 percent of the white men and 4 percent of the black men with health problems in 1966 reported that their problems had existed for less than a year; on the other hand, exactly a third of the whites and half of the blacks reported a duration of ten years or more. Nevertheless, for some, departure from the labor force was attributable to a dramatic change in health condition, or perhaps to an injury. Slightly over a tenth of the dropouts (six whites and five blacks) had reported themselves in "excellent" health in 1966. All these were employed in the survey week, all but two had worked at least fifty weeks in calendar year 1965, and only one had experienced any unemployment in that year. None expected to retire prior to age sixty-two. Yet, all but one of these reported a deterioration in health between the two survey dates, and at least eight of the eleven were forced to quit their jobs for health reasons.[8]

8. Reason for separation was not ascertained in two cases but can reasonably be inferred to have been related to health problems. In only one of the eleven cases was a reason other than health reported for

Our knowledge of the nature of the impairments reported in 1966 by those who subsequently dropped out of the labor force is rather meager. To the query "In what way are you limited?" some of the men responded in functional terms (e.g. "can't walk much"; "have to be careful when I lift"), while others described their health disorders with varying degrees of specificity ("I have arthritis"; "cancer of kidneys"). Nevertheless, a perusal of the fifty-eight specific responses to this question suggests that the problems generally were quite serious. While classification of response is somewhat hazardous, it appears that about sixteen cases involved heart problems of one kind or another and nine involved respiratory problems (emphysema, asthma, "lung trouble"), accounting for over two-fifths of the total. Another third involved arthritis, back problems, and inability to lift, in roughly equal proportions.

Recent Employment Experience

Because chronic health problems are so prominent among the labor force dropouts, it is not surprising that their withdrawals from the labor force were presaged by more spotty employment records in the recent past than prevailed for all men in the labor force in 1966 (Tables 7-III and 7-IV). For example, it was more than twice as common for the labor force dropouts than for the other men to have experienced some periods out of the labor force in calendar year 1965. This was true of more than two-fifths of the dropouts but of less than one-fifth of all of the men. As another measure of the same phenomenon, it may be noted that the average number of weeks out of the labor force in calendar year 1965 for those who withdrew from the labor force between the 1966 and 1967 surveys was in the neighborhood of eleven for both whites and blacks, as compared with less than five weeks for all of the 1966 labor force members of both color groups.

---

quitting the job held in 1966. This individual experienced no worsening of health between the two survey dates. His reason for not being in the labor force during the 1967 survey week was simply that he did "not want to work at this time of year."

TABLE 7-III
COMPARISON OF LABOR FORCE DROPOUTS, 1966–1967 WITH ALL MEN
IN THE LABOR FORCE, 1966, BY COLOR: SELECTED ASPECTS
OF RECENT EMPLOYMENT EXPERIENCE

Characteristic	Proportion of Respondents with Indicated Characteristic	
	Labor Force Dropouts, 1966–1967	All Men in Labor Force, 1966
Unemployed in Survey Week, 1966		
Whites	12.5	1.3
Blacks	16.7	2.3
One or More Weeks of Unemployment, 1965		
Whites	11	11
Blacks	24	19
One or More Weeks Out of Labor Force, 1965		
Whites	43	15
Blacks	48	18

TABLE 7-IV
COMPARISON OF LABOR FORCE DROPOUTS, 1966–1967 WITH ALL MEN
IN THE LABOR FORCE, 1966, BY COLOR: MEAN NUMBER OF WEEKS
EMPLOYED, UNEMPLOYED, AND OUT OF LABOR FORCE, 1965

Labor Force and Employment Status	Mean Number of Weeks in 1965	
	Labor Force Dropouts, 1966–1967	All Men in Labor Force, 1966
Employed		
Whites	37.3	47.7
Blacks	34.5	44.7
Unemployed		
Whites	3.9	1.1
Blacks	6.1	2.7
Out of Labor Force		
Whites	10.8	3.2
Blacks	11.4	4.6

The labor force dropouts had less satisfactory employment records than all men. For example, in the survey week
of 1966, the unemployment rate for all labor force members
was 1.3 percent in the case of whites and 2.3 percent in the
case of blacks. The corresponding rates in the survey week,
however, for those who in the ensuing twelve months were to
withdraw from the labor force were 12.5 and 16.7 percent, respectively. Mean number of weeks of unemployment in calendar year 1965 was also higher for the labor force dropouts
than for all the members of the labor force in 1966 by a ratio
of more than three-to-one in the case of whites and more than

two-to-one in the case of blacks. This apparently resulted from a greater-than-average cumulative duration of unemployment among the dropouts rather than a greater-than-average incidence of unemployment, since there was little difference between the dropouts and others in the proportion experiencing some unemployment in 1965.

These differences suggest that in many cases the observed withdrawal from the labor force between 1966 and 1967 was not a "bolt from the blue" but rather was foreshadowed by previous instances in the recent past. Nevertheless, this point should not be overemphasized. For one thing, a part of the difference in the recent employment record between dropouts and others is doubtless attributable to differences in the occupational composition of the two groups. As has been seen, the dropouts tend to be concentrated in disproportionate numbers in the lower levels of the occupational hierarchy where employment instability is most likely to prevail. The differences between the labor force dropouts and all men that are shown in Tables 7-III and 7-IV would doubtless be smaller if the number of sample cases were large enough to permit controlling for occupation. But even in addition to this point, it is worth noting that a *majority* of the labor force dropouts had not experienced this kind of employment instability in the recent past. More than half of both the white and black dropouts had been in the labor force continuously in calendar year 1965 and about nine-tenths of the whites and three-fourths of the blacks had experienced no unemployment.

Lifetime Work Experience

The less favorable employment record of the labor force dropouts than of all the 1966 labor force members is also evident when one examines the longer-term work histories of the respondents (Table 7-V). The proportion of the dropouts who had served in their 1966 jobs[9] for less than three years was about twice as great as that for all members of the labor force in 1966,

---

9. For those unemployed at the time of the 1966 survey, the reference is to the most recent job.

TABLE 7-V

COMPARISON OF LABOR FORCE DROPOUTS, 1966–1967, AND ALL MEN
IN THE LABOR FORCE, 1966, BY COLOR: PREVIOUS JOB EXPERIENCE

Characteristic	Proportion of Respondents with Indicated Characteristic	
	Labor Force Dropouts, 1966–1967	All Men in Labor Force, 1966
Less Than 3 Years Service in 1966 Job*		
Whites	35	18
Blacks	39	22
10 Years or More Service in 1966 Job*		
Whites	48	61
Blacks	41	56
Was in Best Occupation of Career in 1966* †		
Whites	45	67
Blacks	52	57
Had Been Downwardly Mobile Between First Job and 1966 Job* ‡		
Whites	39	15
Blacks	40	22

* For those unemployed in 1966, data refer to most recent job.
† Respondents were asked in 1966, "I'd like you to think about the best KIND of work you have ever done. What kind of work was that?" The response was compared with the current occupation of the respondent.
‡ Vertical mobility is measured on the basis of the Duncan Socioeconomic Index of Occupations. See Duncan, Otis Dudley: A socioeconomic index for all occupations. In Reiss, Jr., Albert J. *et al.*: *Occupations and Social Status*. New York, Free Press of Glencoe, 1961, pp. 109–38. Downward mobility is defined here as a change of occupations involving a downward change in the first digit of the Duncan Index.

and relatively fewer of the former than of the latter had accumulated as many as ten years of service in that job. Nevertheless, it is noteworthy that almost half of the white and two-fifths of the black dropouts had served that long.

All respondents in the 1966 survey were asked to identify the best occupational assignment of their entire careers. When responses to this question were compared with current occupational assignments, two-thirds of the white members of the labor force and almost three-fifths of the black regarded their current occupational assignment to be the best in which they had ever served. It may be noted in Table 7-V, however, that among those men who were to drop out of the labor force in the ensuing twelve months, the proportions who so regarded their current jobs were somewhat lower (45% for the whites and 52% for the blacks).

Another occupational comparison available for all men in the sample is between the first job they held after leaving school and their current or most recent job in 1966. On the basis of the relative positions of these jobs in the socioeconomic status hierarchy, about 15 percent of the white men and 22 percent of the black men in the labor force in 1966 had slipped down the occupational ladder during the course of their careers. However, among those who were to drop out of the labor force during the next twelve months such examples of downward mobility were considerably more frequent, almost twice as common in the case of the blacks and more than twice as common among the whites. Thus, all the evidence with respect to previous employment experience seems to point in the same direction. While substantial numbers of the labor force dropouts between 1966 and 1967 had been in the mainstream of economic activity in the sense that they had enjoyed stable employment experience and an upward progression among jobs during their careers, larger proportions of them than of men who remained in the labor force had experienced labor market difficulties of one kind or another in both the immediate and more distant past.

Attitudinal Factors

Respondents in the 1966 survey were asked "If, by some chance, you were to get enough money to live comfortably without working, do you think that you would work anyway?" Those who responded affirmatively to this question were classified as having a high commitment to work. About three-fourths of all of the labor force members in 1966 registered high commitment, and in this respect those who later dropped out of the labor force were very little different (Table 7-VI). In the case of the whites, the proportion of labor force dropouts who registered high commitment is only 2 percentage points lower than that for all labor force members in 1966; among blacks the differential is 7 percentage points. It is worth noting in this connection that the labor force dropout group contains a disproportionately large share of farmers and farm laborers,

TABLE 7-VI
COMPARISON OF LABOR FORCE DROPOUTS, 1966–1967, AND ALL MEN
IN LABOR FORCE, 1966, BY COLOR: WORK AND JOB ATTITUDES

	Proportion of Respondents with Indicated Attitude	
Attitude	*Labor Force Dropouts, 1966–1967*	*All Men in Labor Force, 1966*
High Commitment to Work, 1966*		
Whites	76	78
Blacks	67	74
Expected in 1966 to Retire Prior to Age 62		
Whites	19	26
Blacks	10	25
Disliked Job in 1966†		
Whites	18	7
Blacks	18	8

* Respondents classified as having high work commitment are those who responded affirmatively to the question "If, by some chance, you were to get enough money to live comfortably without working, do you think that you would work anyway?" Percentages shown for the labor force dropouts are based on the fifty white men and thirty-four black men who answered this question.

† Based on responses of *employed* men to the question "How do you feel about the job you have now? Do you like it very much, like it fairly well, dislike it somewhat, or dislike it very much?" Percentages relate to those expressing either degree of dislike.

who have above-average commitment to work.[10] The labor force dropouts were twice as likely as all men in the labor force to have farm occupations.

It is also interesting that on the basis of retirement expectations expressed in the 1966 interview those respondents who were subsequently to drop out of the labor force manifested, if anything, a higher attachment to labor market activity than did all men in the labor force. Of the latter about one-fourth of each color group indicated an intention to retire earlier than age sixty-two, but the corresponding proportion among the labor force dropouts was only one-fifth in the case of the whites and one-tenth in the case of the blacks. On the other hand, unfavorable attitudes toward current jobs were more than twice as frequent among those men who subsequently dropped out of the labor force than among all labor force members in 1966. Nonetheless, it is worth noting that less than one in five of the labor force dropouts who were employed in 1966 expressed unfavorable attitudes toward their jobs. By and large, then, on

10. Parnes *et al.: The Pre-Retirement Years*, vol. I, p. 204.

the basis of the attitudinal data shown in Table 7-VI, there would have been little basis for predicting in 1966 which of the labor force members would have withdrawn by 1967. To put this in somewhat different terms, the evidence does not suggest that unfavorable attitudes toward work or job constitute a substantial explanation for the withdrawals from the labor force that occurred between the two years.

IV. PROSPECTS FOR FUTURE LABOR MARKET ACTIVITY

The fact that the men under consideration were not in the labor force during the week preceding the survey in 1967 clearly does not necessarily mean that all of them have permanently withdrawn. Indeed, it has been seen that many of the very same men had periods out of the labor force in 1965. Moreover, we also know that these ninety-eight sample cases who moved out of the labor force between the survey dates in 1966 and 1967 were counterbalanced to some extent by about fifty men who changed their labor force status in the opposite direction.[11] It is therefore pertinent to attempt to draw some conclusion about the future labor force prospects of the group under consideration.

Unfortunately, the available data do not permit this question to be answered conclusively, although they do offer some substantial clues. Five questions were asked of men out of the labor force in the 1967 survey that shed some light on the matter: the date last worked, reason for having left last job, future job-seeking intentions, reason for not looking for work currently, and reaction to a hypothetical job offer.[12] Information on date last worked permits us to ascertain to what extent the

---

11. These men, incidentally, have many of the same characteristics as the dropout group. That is, compared with the men who were in the labor force in 1966, they are older, less likely to be married, less likely to be in white-collar occupations, and much more likely to have health problems. Little more than half the whites and a tenth of the blacks had worked as many as twenty-six weeks during the twelve months preceding the 1967 interview.

12. "If you were offered a job by some employer in this area do you think you would take it?"

labor force dropouts may have been men who were simply enjoying a week or so of fishing between jobs. The data in Table 7-VII indicate that to the extent that such individuals are included among the dropouts, their numbers are relatively small. A large majority of the respondents (82 percent of the whites and 74 percent of the blacks) had not worked for at least three months prior to the 1967 survey. The mean number of weeks out of the labor force during the twelve-month period preceding the 1967 survey was 31.1 for the white men and 32.6 for the black men.

TABLE 7-VII

SELECTED MEASURES OF WORK EXPERIENCE SINCE 1966 SURVEY OF MEN WHO DROPPED OUT OF LABOR FORCE BETWEEN 1966 AND 1967, BY COLOR

(Percentage Distributions)

Measure	*Whites*	*Blacks*
Date Last Worked		
May 1967	6	15
April 1967	12	12
January–March 1967	12	12
June–December 1966	70	62
Total Percent	100	100
Total Number Reporting	33	26
Reason Left Last Job*		
Voluntary Quit: Health	67	71
Layoff	17	10
Other	16	19
Total Percent	100	100
Total Number Reporting	30	21
Mean Number of Weeks in Labor Force in 12 Months Prior to 1967 Survey	20.9	19.4

* Includes only those employed in 1966 survey week.

Unfortunately, there are substantial numbers of nonresponses to the questions relating to reason for leaving last job, reason not currently looking for work, future job-seeking intentions, and reaction to the hypothetical job offer. However, if those for whom information is available are representative, it is doubtful that many of the men who dropped out of the labor force between the two survey dates will resume regular participation in the future. Of those responding to the question, four-fifths of the whites and almost nine-tenths of the blacks explain their failure to look for work in the 1967 survey week on the basis of health problems. Over two-fifths of both the whites and blacks

TABLE 7-VIII
SELECTED INDICATORS OF PROSPECTS FOR FUTURE LABOR
MARKET ACTIVITY BY MEN WHO DROPPED OUT OF LABOR
FORCE BETWEEN 1966 AND 1967, BY COLOR
(Percentage Distributions)

Indicator	Whites	Blacks
Reason Not Looking for Work in 1967 Survey Week		
Health	82	88
Other	18	12
Total Percent	100	100
Total Number Reporting	33	25
Whether Intends to Seek Work in Next 12 Months		
Yes, Definitely	15	20
Yes, Probably	12	0
Depends on Health	15	20
Depends on Other	3	4
Don't Know	9	12
No	47	44
Total Percent	100	100
Total Number Reporting	34	25
Reaction to Hypothetical Job Offer*		
Would Definitely Take Job	4	15
Depends	16	15
No, Because of Health	66	61
No, Other Reason	14	9
Total Percent	100	100
Total Number Reporting	44	33

* Based on responses to the following question: "If you were offered a job by some employer in this area, do you think you would take it?"

who responded to the question on work-seeking intentions during the next twelve months replied categorically in the negative, while only one-fourth of the whites and one-fifth of the blacks said that they would look for work. Of those responding to the hypothetical job offer, four-fifths of the whites and seven out of ten of the blacks said that they would not take such a job, and health problems explained over four-fifths of these negative responses.

But what about the individuals who appear not to have health problems that affect their work? There are fifteen men in the sample (ten whites and five blacks) who reported in 1966 that they had no health limitations affecting their work and who in 1967 indicated that their health was either the same or better than it had been in 1966. This group of respondents appears to differ quite substantially from the others; because of nonresponses, however, their characteristics have to be inferred on the basis of between eight and ten sample cases. In any event, the amount of time they had spent out of the labor force in the twelve months between surveys was twenty-one weeks as compared with about thirty-one for the total group of labor force dropouts. Moreover, all but one said they would take a job if offered one and all but two said they intended to look for work within the next twelve months. The exceptions were one white man who reported his status as "retired" and one black man who explained his current failure to look for work on the grounds that there was no work available for him. Whether most of these men in good health will actually move back into the labor force and be able to find employment remains to be seen. All that can be said at this juncture is that their prospects for doing so appear to be considerably better than those of the remainder of the men.

V. SOME PROTOTYPES

Despite the overwhelming importance of health problems in explaining departures from the labor force between the 1966 and 1967 surveys, there is nevertheless a rich variation in the circumstances surrounding withdrawal. Several prototypic case studies may be considered in greater detail.

Voluntary Retirement

Virtually unique among the ninety-eight cases is the one that may be described as normal early retirement. This fifty-nine-year-old man had been a manager in an electric light and power company for ten years. Employed in the survey week of 1966, he had worked fifty-two weeks during the calendar year 1965. Although he reported liking his job very much in 1966 and although he rated his health as "good" and reported no health problems affecting his ability to work, he nevertheless expected to retire at age sixty. His health remained the same between the dates of the two surveys, but he had quit his job and had been out of the labor force for thirty weeks by the time of the 1967 survey, with no intention of seeking work in the next year. His explanation was that he was "retired." The respondent lived with his wife and had no other dependents. Their total income in the calendar year 1965 was $26,000 and had dropped to $20,000 in 1966. Their net assets at the time of the 1966 survey amounted to $24,000. So far as one can ascertain from the record, here is a case where the individual had simply decided to stop working. At the moment, there are no physical bars to his re-employment. After almost half a year outside the labor force, there is no indication of dissatisfaction with his status.

Progressively Deteriorating Health

As has been seen, most of the persons with health problems who dropped out of the labor force had such problems for considerable lengths of time, and many had experienced periods out of the labor force prior to the current one. An example of this category is provided by the forty-five-year-old self-employed contractor who, although employed in the survey week in 1966, had worked only twenty weeks during calendar year 1965 and only fifteen weeks during the twelve months prior to the 1967 survey. During the remaining weeks in both these periods he had been unable to work. In the 1966 survey he had rated his health as "poor" and reported that it affected his work. He had undergone a spinal operation in 1965 which had resulted in weakness ever since. Between the two surveys his health had worsened. Total family income had been $32,000 in 1965 but only about $10,000 in 1966. He was not seeking work at the time of the 1967 survey for health reasons and reported that whether he looked for work in the next twelve months depended on his health.

Sudden Health Problems

Similar to the above, except that the health problem developed between the two survey dates, is the case of the black fifty-five-year-old self-employed barber who had been employed in 1966, had worked fifty-two weeks in 1965, and had rated his health as excellent in 1966. This individual reported a worsening of health between the two survey dates that affected his ability to work. As a consequence, he gave up the barbering business in which he had served for the previous twenty-two years. Whether he looked for work within the next twelve months, he reported, would depend on his health. At the time of the 1966 survey, his total net assets were slightly under $20,000.

Unemployment, Poor Health, and Discouragement

In a majority of cases in which poor health produced a move out of the labor force, the individual actually found it necessary to quit a job. There are other cases, however, in which the move out of the labor force appears to be attributable to a combination of job loss and poor health which limits reemployability. Illustrative is the case of the fifty-three-year-old black man who had been employed during the survey week of 1966 and who had worked fifty-two weeks in 1965. In the 1966 survey he reported his health as "fair" and referred to a health condition affecting his work, namely, "legs hurt so can't walk much." Nevertheless, between the two surveys he worked twenty-six weeks as a farm laborer until he was laid off. He was not seeking work at the time of the 1967 survey because he believed that no work was available and he had no job-seeking intentions in the next twelve months.

The most extreme case of this kind is that of a fifty-nine-year-old white man who had been unemployed during the survey week of 1966 and who had suffered forty weeks of unemployment during calendar week 1965. His last job at that time had been as an operative at $1.25 per hour, a job in which he had served for less than a year. Between the two survey dates he was out of the labor force entirely. His health, which he had rated poor in 1966 and which had then affected his ability to work, worsened between the dates of the two surveys. In describing his health problems, he referred to "bad heart, emphysema, asthma, and bad back." These severe health problems, his limited education (less than five years) and his age make it exceedingly unlikely that this individual will again find employment.

Temporary Withdrawal

There are some cases in which the probabilities appear to be high that the individual will at least attempt to find work in the future. For example, a fifty-three-year-old unmarried man had been employed in the survey week of 1966 as a semiskilled worker in the construction industry. In calendar year 1965 he had worked forty-four weeks and had been unemployed eight weeks. Between the two surveys he had worked forty-five weeks but had then been laid off and had been unemployed for seven weeks. He had characterized his health as good in the 1966 interview. By 1967 it had worsened but did not, nevertheless, limit the amount or kind of work he could do. His failure to be looking for work in the survey week was attributed to "personal or family reasons" but he definitely planned to seek a job in the next twelve months.

A second case, in which the probability of re-employment appears to be somewhat smaller, is that of a forty-six-year-old black construction laborer who had been employed in the survey week of 1966 and who during 1965 had worked thirty-five weeks, been unemployed fourteen weeks, and been out of the labor force three weeks. Between the two surveys he had worked forty weeks and been unemployed twelve weeks. His health had been only "fair" in 1966 and had limited his ability to work in some unspecified way. Moreover, he reported in 1967 that his health had worsened during the previous twelve months. Nevertheless, his voluntary separation from his last job was not attributed to poor health, even though this is a factor which he mentioned in explaining his failure to be looking for work at the time of the 1967 survey. His principal health problem was arthritis. He definitely expects to look for work within the next twelve months.

VI. SUMMARY

This study has focused on representative samples of middle-aged white and black men who were either working or looking for work when interviewed in the summer of 1966 but who approximately a year later were not. Our purpose has been to explore the circumstances under which these changes in labor force status occurred and to ascertain the extent to which they represent irreversible moves out of the labor force.

It is clear that hardly any of the cases were voluntary retirements in the conventional sense. Over four-fifths said that they were not looking for work because of poor health. While this is not a surprising finding in the light of the evidence produced by previous cross-sectional studies, the longitudinal nature of the present data permit us to be more confident than we otherwise could be that poor health is actually a cause of, rather than a mere rationalization for, withdrawal from the labor force. We know, for example, that even at the time they were in the labor force in 1966 about three-tenths of those who later dropped out reported their health as "poor," in contrast to fewer than one in twenty of all of the labor force members at that time. Six-tenths of the dropout group reported a health problem that limited the amount or kind of work they could do, a proportion three times as high as that which prevailed among all labor force members.

It is also worthy of note that the men who were to drop out of the labor force between 1966 and 1967 registered no weaker commitment to work in the former year than all men in the labor force at that time. Two-thirds of the black men and three-fourths of the white said that they would wish to continue to work even if they were to get enough money to live comfortably without working—proportions that differed very little from those prevailing among all of the labor force members in 1966. Indeed, the proportion of the dropouts who expected in 1966 to retire prior to age sixty-two was only about one-tenth in the case of the blacks and two-tenths in the case of the whites, proportions smaller than those that prevailed among all labor force members.

While for a slight majority of the labor force dropouts withdrawal was a sudden interruption in a pattern of steady work, for very many it was presaged by sporadic labor market activity in the past. For example, over two-fifths of the dropouts had experienced some time out of the labor force in 1965 in contrast with under one-fifth of all labor force members in 1966.

Where poor health is responsible for withdrawal from the labor force it commonly compels a man to quit his job, often one in which he has had a long period of service. However, a not uncommon pattern is one in which unemployment and poor health combined, sometimes with the additional disadvantage of limited education, are responsible for the withdrawal. In some instances of labor force withdrawal, a man in poor health loses his job for reasons which have nothing to do with his health condition; withdrawal from the labor force in these cases appears to be attributable more to the limited re-employment prospects of such a man than to the fact that he is literally unable to work. In this connection, it is noteworthy that labor force dropouts are considerably less likely than those who remain in the labor force to be white-collar workers and are somewhat more likely to have limited education. Thus, they tend to be in those types of jobs in which a given physical limitation is likely to pose a more serious barrier to work.

For some of the labor force dropouts there will doubtless be future periods of work activity. A small minority (less than one-fifth of those responding to the question) indicated in 1967 a definite intention of seeking work within the next twelve months. On the other hand, well over two-fifths answered categorically that they had no such intentions. Moreover, any interruption in employment for the age group of men under consideration is hazardous in view of the disinclination of many employers to hire older workers. In view of this and in view of the serious health problems that so many of the men have, one cannot be sanguine about the possibility of many of them becoming reemployed in the future. We shall want to continue to follow the present sample during the remaining years of the longitudinal study to see how they fare and to ascertain under what circumstances they can successfully reenter the mainstream of economic activity.

Chapter 8

SOME MEDICAL ASPECTS
OF UNEMPLOYMENT

SIDNEY COBB AND STANISLAV V. KASL

In a current study we are looking at the physiology, the
health, and the mental health of blue collar workers whose
jobs have been terminated. With the help of the United Auto
Workers Union, we found factories that were about to close,
interviewed male workers before their jobs were abolished, and
followed the progress of the men for two years afterward.

Four preliminary scientific papers have been published[1]
and Alfred Slote has published a book describing the first
plant closing.[2] In his book, entitled *Termination: The Closing
at Baker Plant,* Slote has managed to capture the feeling of

Note: This research has been supported by grants from the Health Services and
Mental Health Administration (5-R01-CD-00102, 5-R01-HS-00010, K3-MH-
16709, K5-MH-16709).
1. Cobb, Sidney, Brooks, George W., Kasl, Stanislav V., and Connelly,
Winnifred E.: The health of people changing jobs: A description of a
longitudinal study. *Am J Public Health, 56(9):* 1476–1481, Sept. 1966.
Cobb, Sidney, McFarland, David, Kasl, Stanislav V., and Brooks,
George W.: On the relationship among variables in a longitudinal
study of people changing jobs, *Proceedings of the International Epidemiological Association,* Belgrade, Yugoslavia, Savremena Adminis-
tracija, 1970.
Kasl, Stanislav V., Cobb, Sidney, and Brooks, George W.: Changes in
serum uric acid and cholesterol levels in men undergoing job loss,
JAMA, 206: 1500–1507, Nov. 11, 1968.
Kasl, Stanislav V., and Cobb, Sidney: Blood pressure changes in men
undergoing job loss: A preliminary report, *Psychosom Med, 32(1):*
19–38, Jan.-Feb., 1969.
2. Slote, Alfred: *Termination: The Closing at Baker Plant,* New York,
Bobbs-Merrill, 1969.

the whole experience of the death of a plant. There will be further reports on the scientific aspects of the study; and later, there will be a book describing the major results of our set of studies. The present report is an impressionistic and evaluative summary of the trends that are appearing in the data.

The set of studies involved two plant closings. The first took place in a large city and is described in the book *Termination*. The second was in a town of only 2,200 people, thus providing some urban/rural contrast as well as replication. A third scheduled closing never occurred, so we have observed an appreciable group of men through an extended period of anticipated job termination. In addition we observed a control group from several situations of stable employment. The studies focused on married men aged forty to fifty-nine who had at least five years seniority. We selected married men because of their added responsibility, and we chose the older age group because of empirical evidence that older men experience more trouble getting employment. We were quite successful in getting men with a previously stable work experience; for example, in the Baker plant the average seniority among the men in our study was nineteen years.

In looking at the men's experiences, it is convenient to analyze three temporal stages. The first is the period of "anticipation" which extended from the time the closing was first announced to the time it actually took place. The second is the period of "termination and unemployment" which ran from the closing date to approximately thirteen weeks later. Obviously not all the men could be seen immediately after termination, but they were all seen within thirteen weeks, on the average during the sixth week. Of course some men experienced no unemployment; such men were only a lucky few. The third period, "readjustment," is variable in length, but for many men it extended to a year or more beyond the termination and often involved several job changes. Most of the men we observed, however, found a new equilibrium within twenty-four months after the shutdown. The men in this study were interviewed in their homes by public health nurses before the closing, as soon as possible after the closing, and during the period of readjustment at twelve months and then twenty-four months after the closing.

Having given this brief description of the study, we can turn to a few of the physiological variables. We cannot tell you the whole story because only a few of the variables have been analyzed.

First, we studied changes in the level of uric acid. None of our men developed the disease gout, but uric acid in high concentration is the cause of gout. When deposited in the joints, uric acid causes the acute pain characteristic of that disease. During the anticipation phase before the layoff, the uric acid level was substantially and significantly raised, and if this phase had been continued for longer, some cases of gout might have developed. Fortunately, as the men were re-employed uric acid levels returned to normal promptly. For the moment we do not have the exact explanation for this phenomenon, but we are seeking it in further studies.

Turning to blood pressure, we found that both systolic and diastolic pressures were significantly higher during the periods of anticipation, unemployment, and probationary re-employment than during the later period of stabilization on the new job. The size of the drop in blood pressure was related to the perceived severity of unemployment, to the size of the drop in irritation during the period, and inversely to the level of ego resilience. Therefore we might presume that those who had the least ego resilience, the most disagreeable experience, and the most irritation had the greatest elevation of blood pressure during the stressful period. In addition, there was a tendency for blood pressures to rise as the termination date approached; following termination those who got new jobs before the next visit had a significant drop; and those who were unemployed at the next visit had a significant rise in pressure. The changes were not large but were of the order of magnitude of the change resulting from ten years of aging. These findings are based on the analysis of the Baker Plant plus preliminary analysis of the termination in the rural area.

Changes in cholesterol are of interest because of the well-known relationship of high cholesterol levels to frequent coronary heart disease. In contrast to uric acid and blood pressure, cholesterol did not seem to be significantly elevated during the period of anticipation but did rise with unemployment and fell with stabilization.

Thus we see that physiologic changes do take place and that, although the changes on the average are small, the changes for some men are large enough to have potentially serious consequences in terms of gout, hypertension, and coronary heart disease. It is important to emphasize the word *potentially*, because we saw no cases of gout and could not detect an excess of coronary heart disease deaths; but we did see an excess of people needing treatment for hypertension among those who went through the termination experience.

To date, examination of the psychological variables is just in a preliminary stage. However, the nurses brought back a clinical impression that those experiencing termination were depressed, as was suggested by Marie Jahoda Lazarsfeld in her study[3] of a plant closing in an Austrian village. We have a suggestion, not statistically significant, that there was an excess of suicide during the period around the closing of the plant. There were two completed suicides, giving a rate about thirty times the rate expected among blue collar men of this age. In addition we know of one man who threatened suicide and another who presumably made an attempt. Since suicide is known to be a correlate of severe depression, this is suggestive evidence.

Although our direct measures of depression do not show significant changes, two related measures suggest that all those experiencing termination were low on self-evaluation. When asked "How much money should a man with your experience and background be making?" the terminees fixed the rate consistently lower than the controls did, all through the first year. The terminees began to move their estimated rate back toward that of the controls twenty-four months after the termination. Similarly, when asked to evaluate their life situation and future

3. Lazarsfeld, Marie Jahoda: *Die Arbeitslosen von Marienthal*, Leipsig, Germany, S. Hirzel, 1933.

chances for security on an index of a dozen items, the terminees started lower than the controls and lowered their own evaluation as time went on, even after being re-employed. The terminees reacted as if their experience had permanently uprooted optimistic evaluations of their life and of their future.

We noted a few specific illnesses; for example, we saw a fair number of frank cases of hypertension. In fact, hypertension was the most common reason for referring a man to his doctor for treatment and removing him from the analysis (obviously we could not stand by and let a man get progressively sicker with a life-endangering disease). We have now an unsubstantiated impression that much of the problem may have centered around the aggravation of pre-existing hypertension. This hypothesis will of course be tested in the final analysis.

The preliminary analyses also suggest that symptoms of peptic ulcer were unduly common around the time of the termination. This seemed to involve flare-ups of old ulcers as well as the appearance of new ones. In fact, we even found an apparent excess of ulcers in the wives. While in the homes collecting data on the husbands, we found out about three wives who, in the four-month period surrounding the termination, were hospitalized with peptic ulcers. This is an extraordinarily high incidence of ulcers in women, and yet it is presumably an underestimate because the data on this point were not gathered systematically.

We were interested also in arthritis and thus watched for swollen joints and other arthritic manifestations. This matter has not been fully examined; but in the first company to close, there was a distinct excess of joint swelling during the months immediately following the closing. We did not see so much joint swelling in the second company, but the analysis has not yet proceeded to the point where we can tell if this is a real difference or simply a difference in sensitivity of the staff working in the two areas.

There are impressions that more common illnesses such as colds and "intestinal flu" increased in frequency, but this will be difficult to separate from the increase in complaints that we know occurred. Not only did those who lost their jobs have increased complaints, during anticipation, termination, and readjustment, but also they sought more medical care and used more medicines than did the controls. Clearly there was some increase in real illness. We suspect that there was also an increase in complaining and in seeking medical treatment that was out of proportion to the actual illness, but this may be hard to prove from the data we have.

The case of the man that Alfred Slote has called "big Dave Maziak" illustrates many of these points. He stood 6'2" in his socks and at one time was the strongest man in the plant. His status had been based on the fact that he could handle a big paint drum by himself: not just tip it up and roll it around but lift it and place it where he wanted it. Two years before the plant closed, about the time of the second letter saying that the plant definitely would close, he fell between the loading dock and a truck he was unloading. He hurt his back and was sent to a physician. In addition to the back injury, he was found to have diabetes and hypertension. As a result he was put on limited duty and demoted to janitor (a cut in pay of $.40 per hour). He thus lost the principal source of his self-esteem for he could no longer be the strong man of the plant. Instead he was just a guy pushing a broom, in the yard.

When the plant finally closed two years later, much of Maziak's muscle had turned to fat. His blood pressure was higher, and he began to have headaches during the period of termination. Then he developed rheumatoid arthritis. Somehow, he never could manage his medical care appropriately. He seldom kept his medical appointments and often neglected to get his prescriptions filled. When he had the appropriate medications, he often forgot to take them. It was almost as if he thought he was not worthy of the medical care that was being offered him. His self-esteem fell so low that he came to believe that he was not good enough to hold a job. The ultimate manifestation of his depression was a threat of suicide.

During the two years following the closing, Maziak never held a job for more than a few days at a time and most of the jobs that he had were only part-time. He is still surviving as a man at large in society because he is married to a widow who has some insurance income, because he owned his house at the time of the closing, and because his wife had a part-time job. He is a fat, toothless wreck of a man who is disabled by diabetes, hypertension, and arthritis. He is now well beyond rehabilitation, but we believe firmly that he could have been saved by appropriate action.

In the first place, Maziak might have been better handled at the time of his injury. We are not sure that a permanent change to light work was really necessary, but, assuming that it was, at the very least someone in the system should have realized what a demotion to light work would mean to this man. Maziak should have received some help in dealing with this terrible threat to his self-esteem.

In the second place, before termination, Maziak's potentially serious problem might have been recognized. We have ample evidence that persons with physical disabilities, especially those with job restrictions, have much difficulty finding a new job. Big Dave belonged to a group which needs special help, but he received no help whatsoever.

Finally, even some months after the closing, Maziak could have been helped, perhaps not completely rehabilitated but at least helped, by some strong social support. Strong support from his wife, a friend, a neighbor or even a professional counselor could have helped considerably. Unfortunately, even his wife and his physician tended to run him down rather than boost his ego. From our acquaintance with him, it certainly seems that there was a point at which he was ready to fit into almost any niche the community offered, as long as his need to be valued could be met. That point passed and he allowed his blood pressure to mount to dangerous levels (230/120 when last seen) despite the fact that he understood the danger and knew what to do about it. It was almost as though he was intentionally committing suicide by degrees.

Admittedly very few were hit as hard as Maziak, and some even secured better jobs. All acknowledged that the transition was tough.

What can be done to ease the transition? At this point recommendations have to remain a bit tentative because we have not yet completed the analysis; but three things impress us as important. Recommendations on a broader range of problems are presented in testimony before the United States Senate Special Committee on Aging.[4]

Not one of these men was ever hungry, but those over fifty-five years of age generally lost their pensions. Portable pensions are a must for the protection of older workers whose jobs are abolished. The Teachers Insurance and Annuity Association, which provides portable pensions for academic people, is a good model. We cannot understand why unions have not worked toward this more vigorously.

It is clear that people going through this kind of experience need more medical care, yet this is a period during which most men have no health insurance. They usually feel that they do not have the money to continue their insurance at the increased rates set for individual subscribers. So at a time when they have increased demand for service, they have no way to get it. It is our view that health insurance should be an automatic part of unemployment compensation, and there is some reason to believe that this may happen soon.

The above two points are straightforward and it is obvious that society can do something about them. However, the two points are trivial compared with the real issue: the anxiety, anger and depression that result from job loss, we believe, are associated with physiological changes that contribute to illness and contribute directly to an increased tendency to seek medical treatment. We are convinced that the solution to these problems is an interpersonal matter involving active expression of concern and continuous reinforcement of the point that the man is not to be blamed for his temporary misfortune. This should involve the family, the union, the company, and the community.

4. U.S. Congress, Senate, Hearings before the Subcommittee on Employment and Retirement Incomes of the Special Committee on Aging: *Economics of Aging: Toward A Full Share in Abundance,* 91st Cong. 1st sess., 1970, pp. 1203–1217.
See also: U.S. Congress, Senate; *Economics of Aging: Toward A Full Share in Abundance,* 91st Cong. 2nd sess., 1970, pp. 162–166.

We have preliminary evidence that those men whose wives took a psychologically supportive position and did not change their roles fared better from several standpoints than did those men whose wives simply went out and got a job. Incidentally, when the wife could find a job while the husband was unemployed, there was presumably a strong potential for lowering his self-esteem. He might quite naturally, and probably did, feel inadequate in his assigned role of family provider as a result of this reversal.

The unions surely can do something for their members who are temporarily unemployed. The union is for many blue collar workers the principal organization to which they belong and yet it seemed to the men in our study that after the last check-off was taken from their pay the union abandoned them. We have the impression that the men were right because instead of increasing activity on behalf of those in trouble the union simply left the men entirely alone. This can be construed as meaning "Now that you are out of work you are not worth fussing over." We do not see why the unions cannot take some responsibility for their members who happen to be between jobs and therefore are unable to pay dues. The unions, in the process of working on what they consider more important tasks, tend to lose sight of the importance of simple humanity.

In any closing, the company in question has a real responsibility for employees; but on the whole, the company officials are more concerned with the stockholder's money than with their employee's health. In some senses, this attitude of company officials is appropriate to their managerial function because every business manager knows that his first duty is to make money for the company. Since money is the issue, financial pressure will probably have to be brought to bear on company management. It has ben eour observation that severance pay is really very detrimental to the workers, for it forces them to leave at the convenience of the company, not at a time suitable for them to make an orderly transfer to a new job. We believe that in the long run the employees would be better off and the company would lose little if it arranged for flexible termination during a period of thirty to ninety days, rather than giving severance pay for termination on the day most convenient to the company. This would permit a man to leave the dying plant when his next employer is ready for him. Surely that is a humane approach, but it is probable that nothing will be done until enlightened unions impress this fact upon companies planning to close. Perhaps a substantial fee paid to the union welfare fund for each man still unemployed at the end of the termination period would encourage the company managers to work hard at helping the men find new jobs.

Finally, at the community level there are improvements that can be made. For example, the men in our study soon learned that the employment agencies would not help them until they had actually terminated. Worse than that, government retraining programs were not available to them until they were out of work or already re-employed on a new job for which they were inadequately trained. We submit that this is an inhumane way to run employment and training agencies and hope that these policies will soon be changed.

The emergency nature of Dave Maziak's situation should have been recognized before termination; but even without his disability, his situation should have been looked on as an emergency when he passed six weeks of unemployment. Six weeks seems to be a reasonable estimate of the time when serious secondary effects begin to occur; for after repeated rejections, a man begins to believe that he is not good enough to hold a job. This must be prevented lest each factory closing add appreciably to the rolls of the permanently unemployable.

We feel strongly that we should not legislate against change or progress. Rather we should learn to deal openly, honestly, humanely and constructively with the problems that are created by factory closings or changes to automation. If we fail, there will be a demand for protection of the status quo and thus an inhibition of industrial progress.

IV. PSYCHOLOGICAL DATA AND
THE IMPLICATIONS FOR COUNSELING

THE AGE-INTELLIGENCE RELATIONSHIP— LONGITUDINAL STUDIES CAN MISLEAD

RUSSEL F. GREEN AND GUNARS REIMANIS[1]

For many years there has been a widespread belief that the intellectual or cognitive powers of individuals tend to increase until perhaps the early to middle twenties and then to decline slowly thereafter. Several studies reported during the past fifteen years tend to contradict this belief. Each study in turn suffered from one or more deficiencies. A study by Green[2] probably produced the best evidence to date that intellectual powers, as measured by intelligence tests such as the Wechsler Adult Intelligence Scale, do not decline before age sixty-five.

If indeed it is true that intellectual powers of individuals typically remain intact until age sixty-five, then it is quite important for employers, vocational counselors, employment counselors, all who are concerned wtih the employment of individuals who are between the ages of forty and sixty-five, to be aware of this fact and to take it into account as they hire, counsel, and explore retraining possibilities.

The study described below was carried out because the 1969 study by Green contradicted an earlier study by Berkowitz and Green.[3] This means that the senior author of this paper is

Note: The Veterans Administration provided most of the financial support for this study.

1. During the period of the study Dr. Reimanis was a research psychologist, part time, on the Veterans Administration Center staff at Bath, N.Y.
2. Green, Russel F.: Age-intelligence relationships between ages sixteen and sixty-four: A rising trend. *Dev Psychology, 1:* 618–627, 1969.
3. Berkowitz, Bernard, and Green, Russel F.: Changes in intellect with age: 1. Longitudinal study of Wechsler Bellevue scores. *J Genet Psychol, 103:* 3–21, 1965.

in the interesting position of having been author and coauthor, respectively, of two earlier articles dealing with the age-intelligence relationship which presented almost completely opposite results. The ambiguous situation represents, in miniature, the situation in the general literature. If general acceptance for either outcome is to be achieved, it is therefore necessary to determine *why* opposing results occur. Thus this study was undertaken to attempt to reconcile the differences between the two earlier ones.

The Wechsler-Bellevue (W-B) and the Wechsler Adult Intelligence Scale (WAIS) were used in the three studies, the latter scale being an updated version of the former. Each is individually administered, each has eleven subtests of various kinds, and each produces a verbal I.Q., a Performance I.Q., and a Full-Scale I.Q. For each, the raw scores are converted to scaled scores derived from a reference group consisting of a representative sample of persons aged twenty to thirty-four. The scaled scores are then converted to I.Q. scores for each five- or ten-year age band, depending on the ages involved. The scores used for investigating age differences then have to be the scaled scores.

PREVIOUS RESULTS

In their 1963 study, Berkowitz and Green published the results of a longitudinal study of changes in W-B intelligence test performance in an aging population. The subjects were long-term residents of a Veteran's Administration domiciliary. Their mean age was 56.3 at the first testing and 65.0 at the second. Mean scaled scores declined on every subtest, and by approximately the same relative amounts. After what seemed to be a sufficient investigation of reading and other signs of apparently normal and continuing cognitive activities, *it was suggested that the decline could reasonably be attributed to the aging process.*

In the 1969 study, Green published another investigation of the age-intelligence relationship. One set of subjects was a stratified random sample from the population of Puerto Rico between the ages of sixteen and sixty-four, inclusive. Stratification was on urban-rural residence and on region of the island. All other variables, including age, were allowed to appear at random. The sample had been drawn to standardize the Spanish language WAIS (EIWA). A second set of subjects was made up by combining the subjects in four of the standardization age strata with additional subjects randomly drawn from the same four strata (25–29, 35–39, 45–49, and 55–64). Sufficient additional cases were drawn to make it possible to set up matched education distributions within the four age strata, so that education would be at least partially controlled in an age-intelligence study.

The standardization sample showed the typically-observed decline of scaled scores with age. These results are shown in Figures 9–1 and 9–2. From Figures 9–3 and 9–4, on the other hand, it is clear that *the education-balanced groups showed no significant decline in performance with age in any of the three total scores.*

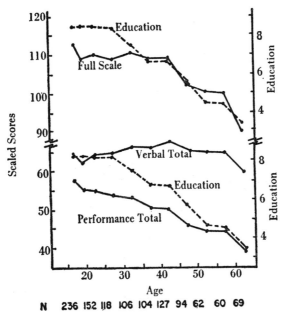

Figure 9–1. Age-mean scaled score relationships in the total standardization sample of 1,127.

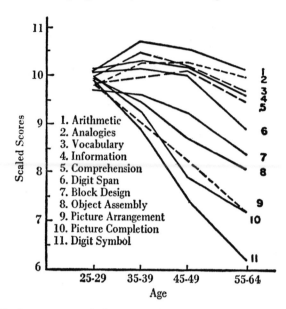

Figure 9–2. Age-mean scaled score relationships of the eleven subtests of the standardization sample. (Age groups corresponding to education-balanced groups.)

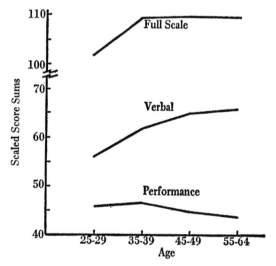

Figure 9–3. Education-balanced groups. (Age-adjusted mean relationships after covariance adjustments for urban-rural residence and for education.)

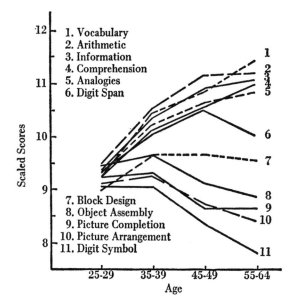

Figure 9–4. Education-balanced groups. (Age-adjusted mean relationships after covariance adjustments of the eleven subtests.)

In fact, continued growth occurred in the verbal total to about age forty-nine and never showed loss.[4]

These results justified a new analysis of the standardization sample data. Variance due to education was covaried out of the age-score function. This second analysis produced exactly the same results as the analysis of the education-balanced groups. From these and other results it was concluded: first, that the typical decline results are attributable to the fact that age groups have progressively more formal education as the years go by, and second that the amount of formal education is a surprisingly strong determinant of one's level of cognitive functioning for most if not all the rest of his life.

Why did the longitudinal study show decline in mean full-scale scores, while the stratified random sample, when more adequately analyzed to control for age differences in educa-

---

4. The Digit-Symbol substitution subtest, a purely speeded function, did show decline with age.

tion, appeared to show stability during the same age span (55 to 64)?

It seemed likely that something had gone astray with the longitudinal study rather than with the stratified random sample study. The Puerto Rican study was clearly representative of a well-defined general population and the results obtained deserved credence. On the other hand, a Veteran's Administration domiciliary is not a representative sample of the adult population, nor is it a normally stimulating place to live. Even so, it had been noted that some of the residents did not show decline, in fact they had actually scored somewhat higher at the second testing, when they were older, than at the first. Some men had obtained and held jobs that involved intellectual activities. Some seemed to remain active in various ways. Might it be that if the men were subdivided according to the amount and kind of their activities, there would be differential declines and that the function of the more active group would be similar to the function of the stratified random sample group in Puerto Rico that was studied later?

Method

The method of approach was again a longitudinal study. Men at the Veteran's Administration Center who had taken either the W-B or the WAIS one or more times at least five years previously were given the same test as before. Almost all men who were under sixty-five had been given the WAIS once previously, and almost all who were sixty-five or older had been given the W-B twice previously. Since the stratified random sample study covered the population only to age sixty-four, the men were divided into two groups in the new study— those sixty-five and over and those sixty-four and under. The sixty-five and over group had been in residence at the center for an average of about sixteen years; those under sixty-five for an average of six years.

The men were asked to report to the Psychological Service Center, where they were interviewed and asked to cooperate in the testing. The interview was directed at attempting to establish rapport and to elicit information on the kinds of activities in which they engaged. Most of them seemed to respond to this show of interest by cooperating in the testing program. A few who would have been eligible refused to report, however, and therefore were not tested.

Information concerning types and amounts of activities of the men was obtained from the pretesting interviews and the center's files on the men. The files contained records of work assignments, recreational activities, rule infractions, and in some instances other information growing out of interviews with other center personnel. The two sets of information were coded and then each set was rated independently by the two authors. There were, then, four sets of ratings. The ratings were made on a four-point scale, from *one*, representing virtually no identifiable cognitive activity, to *four*, representing a considerable amount of reading of books and newspapers, going to movies, following newscasts, and so on.[5]

There is a possibility that the preliminary interview included in this study may have resulted in an increased willingness to try harder, at least on the part of some of the men. Among those under sixty-five who were being tested for the second time, motivation might not have been very different during the first and second testings, since the first testing occurred when they entered the center. Men who were not yet acclimated could reasonably be expected to cooperate because they did not yet know what to expect in the way of limits in their new living environment. Among the men being tested for the third time, motivation could conceivably have been more like

---

5. The two raters agreed completely on from 50 to 60 percent of the ratings and either agreed or differed by no more than one on 95 to 100 percent of the ratings. The ratings of the two kinds of information agreed exactly or differed by one in 90 percent of the cases. It seems reasonable, therefore, to assume that the placement of the men was sufficiently accurate for research purposes. The test administrators were two male psychologists with master's degrees and one graduate student in psychology. Previous testing had been done in part by a Ph.D. clinical phychologist and in part by a testing technician under the supervision of a Ph.D. clinical psychologist.

that which prevailed at their first testing than at their second. This observation will be of some importance later.[6]

Summary descriptions of the subjects are presented in Table 9-I.

TABLE 9-I
SUMMARY DESCRIPTIONS OF THE SUBJECTS

	Age 64 or Under at Time of Second Testing (WAIS Test Used)		Age 65 or Over at Time of Third Testing (Wechsler-Bellevue Test Used)		
	1st Testing	*2nd Testing*	*1st Testing*	*2nd Testing*	*3rd Testing*
N—	87–90	86–90	44–46	46	39–46
Mean Years of Education	9.21	9.21	7.37	7.37	7.37
Mean IQ	93.59	95.13	104.5	101.3	101.3
Mean Age	51.73	57.72	57.15	66.17	73.41
Mean Activity Rating		2.53			2.22

RESULTS

The overall test results for the two age groups are presented in Tables 9-II and 9-III.

The results clearly are more similar to the results found in the balanced-education, stratified random sample study than they are to those in the early longitudinal study. The under

6. Some men did not respond to all subtests. A subject would simply announce that it was time for his news show, or whatever, and stop. In other instances a man would say that he could not see well enough or hear well enough and would refuse to complete one or more subtests. The practice adopted was to omit scores for subtests and sometimes for either the verbal or performance totals (and therefore for the full scale), but to keep and use whatever data were obtained whenever at least three subtests for the performance section or four for the verbal section were completed. This gives rise to varying sample sizes and to scale score sums that are not exactly equal to the sums of the subtest scores. It is believed that this practice yields more accurate results than assigning zeros to refused portions or dropping such cases. The reader should bear in mind the fact that W-B and WAIS results are not fully comparable. The W-B data are based on the use of prorated scores for the verbal and full-scale scaled scores. The WAIS standardization dropped this practice. Also, the mean I.Q.'s estimated from the W-B are likely to be higher than those from the WAIS.

TABLE 9-II

WAIS RESULTS FOR GROUP IN WHICH EVERY MAN WAS
UNDER SIXTY-FIVE AT SECOND TESTING

	Testing		*Difference Between Second and First Tests*	*N for Mean Difference*	*SE Difference*
	First	*Second*			
N –	87–90	86–90	84–90		
Test					
Information	9.89	9.64	–.22	90	.114
Comprehension	8.56	8.80	.26	87	.279
Arithmetic	9.28	8.62	–.60*	87	.206
Similarities	6.79	6.91	.08	86	.211
Digit Span	8.87	9.08	.32	85	.271
Vocabulary	9.29	9.71	.43*	89	.134
Digit Symbol Substitution	5.44	5.31	–.17	87	.154
Picture Completion	7.70	7.84	.18	84	.180
Block Design	7.34	6.95	–.39	87	.213
Picture Arrangement	7.06	6.95	–.08	86	.202
Object Assembly	6.59	6.77	.30	85	.257
Verbal Total	52.86	52.78	.25	86	.609
Performance Total	34.16	33.85	–.05	85	.569
Full Scale Total	86.77	86.47	–.16	85	.938
I.Q.	93.59	95.13	1.65	.88	.593

* Statistically significant differences.

sixty-five group showed virtually no decline during the six years between tests. Among the eleven subtests, the arithmetic mean scaled score was significantly lower at the second testing, whereas the vocabulary mean scaled score was significantly higher. No other mean score was different, not even the digit-symbol substitution mean. Neither were the verbal, performance, and total mean scaled scores. Since there are different norms as individuals grow older, this meant that the mean I.Q.'s of these men rose slightly during this period.

The sixty-five-and-over group had taken both previous tests. The first two testings had occurred at average ages of fifty-seven and sixty-six. Every mean scaled score, except information and picture completion, had declined significantly during that time. During the nine years between the first and second testings, the full-scale scaled score declined 9.3 points. During the seven years between the second and third testings, the mean age increased from 66.2 to 73.4 years and the mean full-scale scaled score declined by only four points. During this interval only the picture arrangement, block design, performance total,

TABLE 9-III
W-B RESULTS FOR GROUP IN WHICH EVERY MAN WAS SIXTY-FIVE OR OVER AT THIRD TESTING

N — Test	Testing			Mean Difference		N for Difference		SE Difference	
	First 44–46	Second 46	Third 39–46	Second and First 44–46	Third and Second 39–46	Second and First	Third and Second	Second and First	Third and Second
Information	10.70	10.61	10.30	−.09	−.30	46	46	.248	.236
Comprehension	9.26	8.46	8.07	−.80*	−.42	46	45	.362	.384
Digit Span	7.48	6.59	6.81	−.89*	.21	46	43	.248	.291
Arithmetic	7.67	6.54	6.45	−1.13*	−.09	46	44	.311	.328
Similarities	7.93	7.15	6.78	−.78*	−.37	46	46	.304	.400
Vocabulary	10.59	9.14	9.26	−1.17*	.12	46	46	.177	.163
Verbal Total	44.80	40.74	40.17	−3.82*	−.57	46	46	.629	1.021
Picture Arrangement	6.71	6.00	5.15	−.80*	−.85*	45	41	.339	.306
Picture Completion	8.50	8.35	7.93	−.15	−.42	46	43	.375	.353
Block Design	7.04	6.00	5.10	−1.04*	−.90*	46	39	.246	.276
Object Assembly	9.00	7.02	6.55	−1.98*	−.47	46	42	.435	.466
Digit Symbol Substitution	6.14	4.61	4.08	−1.40*	−.53	44	40	.302	.304
Performance	37.33	31.98	29.09	−5.34*	−2.89*	46	43	1.098	.856
Full-Scale Total	82.13	72.72	68.74	−9.92*	−4.06*	46	43	1.353	1.468
I.Q.	104.52	101.35	101.77	−3.17*	.42	46	43	.984	.815

* Statistically significant differences.

and full-scale total means declined significantly. The average decrease for the earlier period was one point per year and for the later period, .56 of a point per year. Thus the rate of decline was slower during the later period than during the first.

The results derived from dividing the men into subgroups according to their rated levels of cognitive activity are presented in Tables 9-IV and 9-V.

Among the under age sixty-five group (Table 9-IV) it is clear that the more active men tend to have had more education and also higher I.Q.'s. In spite of these differences in education and I.Q., *on no subtest or total score was there any difference in mean rate of change associated with different activity levels.*

For the sixty-five and over group the results were the same as for the under sixty-five group. The one exception was the picture completion subtest, which showed significantly more decline in the less active group between the first two testings and showed significantly less decline in the same group between the second and third testings. Over the entire period they changed by almost the same amount, and therefore it seems likely that the different outcomes on this one subtest in the two periods are not important to the problem being studied here. It is clear that the differences in activity levels that were observable did not mean differential decline.[7]

---

7. A few other results might prove helpful in any review of the adequacy of the data being presented. For instance, in the under sixty-five group, the test-retest correlation of the full scale scores was .92 over the six years between testings. The number of years of education correlated .67 with the full scale scores at the first testing and .62 at the second. These correlations are consistent with results obtained in other studies. In the over sixty-four group, the test-retest correlation of full scale scores was .96 over the 9.2 years between the first and second testings, .93 over the 7.2 years between the second and third testings, and .93 over the 16.3 years between the first and third testing. Number of years of education correlated with the full-scale scores obtained at the first testing, .53 at the second and .51 at the third. Except for the .96 correlation between full scale scores from the first two testings, these correlations all seem to be reasonably consistent with results to be expected. The .96 seems high.

TABLE 9-IV

DIFFERENCES BETWEEN ACTIVITY-RATED GROUPS, ALL MEN UNDER SIXTY-FIVE

Test	First Testing		Sig	Second Testing		Sig	Sig of Difference Between Differences
	Low Activity	*High Activity*		*Low Activity*	*High Activity*		
Information	9.26	10.62	sig	9.00	10.45	sig	NS
Comprehension	7.83	9.46	sig	7.72	10.15	sig	NS
Arithmetic	8.54	10.18	sig	7.86	9.58	sig	NS
Similarities	5.97	8.02	sig	5.76	8.32	sig	NS
Digit Span	8.25	9.64	sig	8.52	9.75	NS	NS
Vocabulary	8.54	10.22	sig	8.75	10.88	sig	NS
Digit Symbol	4.84	6.20	sig	4.69	6.08	sig	NS
Picture Completion	7.08	8.46	sig	4.96	8.92	sig	NS
Block Design	6.88	8.00	sig	6.25	7.82	sig	NS
Picture Arrangement	6.20	8.12	sig	6.06	8.08	sig	NS
Object Assembly	5.81	7.54	sig	5.91	7.85	sig	NS
Verbal Total	48.27	58.10	sig	47.61	59.10	sig	NS
Performance Total	30.89	38.18	sig	29.96	38.74	sig	NS
Full-Scale Total	78.86	96.68	sig	77.57	97.64	sig	NS
I.Q.	88.88	99.46	sig	89.84	101.79	sig	NS
N –	48–50	39–40		48–50	38–40		
Years Between Tests	6.10	5.85		6.10	5.85		
Years of Education	8.37	10.27		8.37	10.27		

TABLE 9-V

DIFFERENCES BETWEEN ACTIVITY-RATED GROUPS, ALL MEN SIXTY-FIVE AND OVER

Test	First Testing		Sig of Difference	Second Testing		Sig of Difference	Third Testing		Sig of Difference	Sig of Difference Between Differences	
	Low A	Hi A		Low A	Hi A		Low A	Hi A		2-1	3-2
Information	9.68	11.90	sig	9.80	11.57	NS	9.24	11.57	sig	NS	NS
Comprehension	8.32	10.38	sig	7.80	9.24	NS	7.29	8.95	NS	sig	sig
Digit Span	7.20	7.81	NS	6.08	7.19	NS	6.08	7.74	NS	NS	NS
Arithmetic	6.60	8.95	NS	5.36	7.95	NS	5.54	7.55	NS	NS	NS
Similarities	6.56	9.57	sig	6.00	8.52	sig	5.64	8.14	sig	NS	NS
Vocabulary	9.56	11.81	sig	8.32	10.71	sig	8.04	10.71	sig	NS	NS
Verbal Total	40.04	50.48	sig	36.24	46.09	sig	35.00	46.33	sig	NS	NS
Picture Arrangement	6.16	7.40	NS	5.20	6.95	sig	4.30	5.95	NS	NS	NS
Picture Completion	7.88	9.24	NS	6.92	10.05	sig	7.05	8.86	NS	sig	sig
Block Design	6.40	7.81	NS	5.68	6.38	NS	4.35	5.89	NS	NS	NS
Object Assembly	8.76	9.29	NS	6.76	7.33	NS	5.78	7.47	NS	NS	NS
Digit Symbol	5.39	6.95	sig	3.92	5.42	sig	2.90	5.25	sig	NS	NS
Performance Total	34.48	40.71	NS	28.48	36.14	sig	25.04	33.33	sig	NS	NS
Full-Scale Total	74.52	91.19	sig	64.72	82.24	sig	58.32	79.76	sig	NS	NS
I.Q.	100.24	109.62	sig	96.76	106.81	sig	96.09	107.71	sig	NS	NS
N—	23-25	20-21		25	21		23-25	19-21		—	—
Age	57.44	56.80	NS	66.08	66.29	NS	73.44	73.38	NS	—	—
Years of Education	6.36	8.57	sig	6.36	8.57		6.36	8.57		—	—

DISCUSSION

The activity levels of the men were related to I.Q., but were not associated with declines in intelligence scores. One can speculate that I.Q. is more likely to be a determinant of activity level than the reverse. This would follow from the failure of activity level to have the anticipated effect on I.Q. Of course, both might be concomitants of various third factors. We might reasonably expect that factors that effect change in I.Q. might also effect change in activity level, but the data were not sufficient to support this possibility. The correlation between I.Q. and activity level apparently is not very high—being estimated at about .3 or so from the data. This leaves ample room for these two variables to be affected differentially by other factors.

It is apparent that measured intelligence-decline in the Veteran's Administration Center population was quite different during the period covered by the second longitudinal study from that during the first. If it is a fact that intellectual decline is negligible before age sixty-five, as the second longitudinal study showed, we need to find a reasonable basis for explaining why the two longitudinal studies came out so differently—especially for men under sixty-five.

The data from the first study were originally analyzed as a single group with no age subdivisions. These data were reanalyzed by age group. The 185 men in the first study were subdivided into age groups 59 and under, 60 to 62, 63 to 64, 65, 66 to 67, 68 to 69, 70 to 71, 72 to 73, and 74 to 79, based on their ages at the time of the second testing. In the group that was fifty-nine and under, the full-scale decline was only 3.56 points. In all other groups except for the oldest, the decline was fairly constant at about ten points. The oldest group showed a 14.7 point decline (see Table 9-VI).

It turns out, then, that the fifty-nine and under group was not as different from the present sixty-four and below group as had appeared. The under fifty-nine group from the first longitudinal study declined by about 3.6 points and the under sixty-five group of the second longitudinal study declined by less

TABLE 9-VI
REANALYSIS OF ORIGINAL LONGITUDINAL STUDY

Age	N	Full Scale			Verbal		Performance	
		First	*Second*	*Difference*	*First*	*Second*	*First*	*Second*
59 and Below	25	86.44	82.88	3.56	47.16	45.08	39.08	37.80
60, 61, 62	17	87.06	76.29	10.76	46.47	41.12	40.59	34.94
63, 64	34	74.82	65.47	9.37	39.15	37.47	38.00	31.91
65	11	78.54	71.54	7.00	41.54	39.27	37.00	32.27
66, 67	28	65.68	55.53	10.13	36.11	31.29	29.57	24.25
68, 69	18	82.28	73.22	9.05	48.83	42.78	36.11	30.44
70, 71	23	71.48	60.00	11.48	41.70	35.70	29.78	24.30
72, 73	15	69.00	57.47	11.53	38.60	33.47	30.40	24.00
74–79	10	77.60	63.90	14.70	43.00	37.80	34.60	25.70
80+	3	(Too few scores to report)						

than a half a point (see Table 9-II). This difference is statistically significant. A check on the comparative declines of the sixty to sixty-four subgroup in the second study shows a very small increment of 1.1 points on the full-scale total compared with the ten points lost by the age sixty to sixty-four group in the first study.

For groups above sixty-five, the differences were consistently larger in the first than in the second study. If one allows for the different number of years between testings, however, the declines do not appear to be so large. Even so, the declines continue to be about .56 of a point per year in the second study and 1 to 1.5 points per year in the first study, depending on the ages of the men.

It is apparent that the outcomes of the two studies were, in fact, different. Decline was greater, and probably abnormally greater, in the first study. Was there a real loss in ability to respond to the test in the first group, or were the lowered scores affected by extraneous factors? For instance, if the men were generally very poorly motivated during the second testing period in the first study, might not this have resulted in lower performance? A review of conditions at the domiciliary during the period shows that it is possible that this did, in fact, occur.

The earlier study group was clearly being affected quite profoundly in ways that the later group was not, especially in the sixty-to-sixty-four group. It is possible that these were the men most affected by the "old soldier's" environment. They were approaching the more or less official retirement age of sixty-five and might have been depressed because there was no apparent hope of returning to a more normal life. The second study group were the recipients of many services which could have encouraged them not to view the sixty-fifth birthday as the end of the road. It seems likely that beneficial results were produced by the changes in environment that were instituted.

SUMMARY

Longitudinal studies are not necessarily more reliable avenues to studying or tracing age-related changes than are other approaches. In this instance, the results of a stratified random sample study suggested that something was wrong with a longitudinal study and initiated the search that helped to resolve the problem.

The second testing period for the first longitudinal study was almost entirely limited to the first half of 1960. It can fairly be said that during most of the 1950's the environment at the center was not as good as it was during most of the 1960's. During 1958, plans were made to improve the living environment at the center by changing its status as an "old soldier's home" to something more adequate. The program included methods of stimulating social interaction among the members, helping the men to adapt to their living quarters, changing to a rehabilitation unit or to a therapeutic community. The object was to revise the whole philosophy of a domiciliary and to implement the philosophy.[8]

The new program could have caused changes in the motivations, attitudes, and expectations of many of the men, especially those who were still under 65—or perhaps even of some who were somewhat older. The results of the two longitudinal studies indicate that the changes probably did have an effect, and probably at all ages up to about seventy.[9]

---

8. A rehabilitation program was initiated. The Social Work Service Unit moved to the domiciliary where it was in much closer contact with the members; a few years later the main domiciliary service also moved to the domiciliary; a new theater and recreational building providing ample space for recreational and other volunteer activities was completed in 1960; the members' Hobby Shop was moved from a dark and crowded basement area to better quarters; domiciliary assistants who became familiar with each man and looked out for his needs were appointed; the living quarters were considerably improved; and starting about 1960, the members had more direct access to vocational counseling, which helped to substitute the feeling that they could get out and get a job for the feeling that they had come there simply to die.

9. The time interval between tests in the second study may not have been long enough for all effects from the first testing to have disappeared. Retesting older men within a six-month period results in about a 3.5 point increment in mean full-scale score. See: Berkowitz, Bernard, and Green, Russel F.: Changes in intellect with age: V. Dif-

The results of the second longitudinal study are in close agreement with the balanced education, stratified random sample study results. There are excellent bases now for stating that in most respects I.Q. test performance does not decline before age sixty-five. This is especially the case with verbal abilities. Performance scores that depend on visual and motor performance do decline, but even here the extent to which this decline may be attributable solely to peripheral changes is not well established.

Finally, it appears that the environment of men in institutions such as a veteran's domiciliary is important to intellectual function. It seems likely that the effects of environment are indirect, operating through motivations, attitudes, and expectations rather than directly on ability to function. This conclusion, of course, is not new. It may be, however, that this bit of evidence will help to reinforce it by providing a factual base upon which others may successfully bring about desirable change.

---

ferential changes as functions of time intervals and original scores, *J Genet Psychol* 107:179–192, 1965. We do not yet know whether, or over what time interval, this effect dissipates. It probably does dissipate with time, even as most learned skills do to some extent if they are not practiced. The two longitudinal studies compared here differed in time interval between testings by about 2.5 years (6 years versus 8.5 years). The difference in time interval might cause some difference in mean change, but is quite unlikely to be a satisfactory explanation for *all* the difference. After all, the sixty to sixty-four group showed a difference in mean change of some ten points between the two studies.

Chapter 10

GENERAL APTITUDE TEST
BATTERY SCORES FOR MEN IN DIFFERENT
AGE AND SOCIOECONOMIC GROUPS

JAMES L. FOZARD AND RONALD L. NUTTALL

This paper summarizes General Aptitude Test Battery (GATB) scores for employed or retired men. The scores are summarized by differences in age and socioeconomic status (SES). Its purpose it to provide vocational counselors with information about the GATB that is not ordinarily available, but which may be useful when the GATB is considered for use in employment counseling of older workers.

While the data to be presented provide a useful supplement to existing information about the GATB, it should be recognized that they do not represent a comprehensive set of norms. The sample on which they are based is rather select, and not typical of the entire working population. The most important value of the scores is that they provide a way for the counselor to enhance his understanding of the effects of differences in age and SES on an individual's performance on the GATB. Secondarily, for those cases where the vocational counselor finds that a client's background is similar to those of individuals represented in the present sample, he may want to evaluate

Note: The research was performed as part of the Boston V.A. Outpatient Clinic Normative Aging Study, Benjamin Bell, M.D., Director. This research was supported in part by the Council for Tobacco Research—USA, and NICHD Grant No. 5R01–HD00340–08 to Harvard Medical School.

Tables 10-I, 10-II, and Figures 10–3, 10–4 are reprinted from Fozard, J.L., and Nuttall, R.L.: General aptitude test battery scores for men differing in age and socioeconomic status. *J Appl Psychol,* 55: 1971, 372–379. Copyright 1971 by the American Psychological Association, and reproduced by permission.

his client's test scores in terms of the normal values presented later.

Before proceeding, three important questions need to be raised and answered. First: why is there a need for aptitude testing of older workers in the first place? One may argue that older workers are generally experienced in one or more occupations, and that their experience can be used as a basis for employment counseling. One answer to this question is that the pattern of occupations in our country is changing at a rapid rate, primarily because of mechanization or other changes in the way that work is performed. Therefore, a man seeking employment may, on the basis of experience, be most qualified for a job that is not open to him. Therefore, the counselor's main task may be to assist the client in selecting alternative occupations and training programs.

A second, and related, answer is that the number of employable older people in our society is increasing. Many of these persons will be seeking "second" or post retirement careers, and aptitude testing will help them assess their potential for a number of occupations.

The second question: why should there be supplemental aptitude test information for older workers? One answer to this question is based on the fact that the average scores on the GATB become lower as age increases. Analyses of the data presented in this article and the results of other studies consistently show this trend for subjects from different occupational and educational backgrounds. As a result, the older individual typically qualifies for fewer Occupational Aptitude Pattern Structures (OAP). For example, the United States Department of Labor reported a study which showed that as age increased from an average of twenty-two to seventy-two years, the average percentage of twenty-three OAP patterns passed systematically declined from 64 percent to 6 percent.[1] Does this mean that, on the basis of his test scores, the older worker is, on the average, really qualified for fewer occupations than younger

1. United States Department of Labor: *Manual for the General Aptitude Test Battery.* Section III: Development. Washington, D.C., Government Printing Office, 1967, p. 223.

workers? We don't know; age differences were not taken into account in the establishment of the OAPs. Many authorities have suggested that OAPs ought to be "corrected" for age, but right now there is no completely satisfactory solution to the problem of what, if any, age adjustments should be made in the OAP scores.[2] Until further information is available, vocational counselors may use information based on the expected aptitude scores for a group of a man's peers in age and occupational status as a basis for vocational guidance.

There is a second answer to the question of why there should be extra GATB data for older workers. It is simply that the effects of age are not uniform for the human abilities measured by the test. For some of the GATB subtests, performance is influenced mostly by differences in occupational status and education rather than by age. In others, the opposite is true, i.e. the effects of age differences are essentially the same for persons who may differ widely in occupational status and educational background. The implication for the counselor is that he should weigh his advice to a client according to the aptitudes which are important for a specific range of occupations.

An additional reason why norms by age and SES are useful to the counselor is that he is often concerned with the speed with which a given client is aging. A man who has abilities much above the age and socioeconomic specific norms is likely to be a better bet for retraining and career shift than is a man of the same age and socioeconomic status who is much below the ability norms of his group. If a client is tested on two oc-

---

2. Droege, R.C.: Effect of aptitude-scores adjustments by age curves or prediction of job performance, *J Applied Psychology, 51:* 181–186, 1967; Hirt, M.L.: Aptitude changes as a function of age. *Personnel and Guidance Journal, 43:* 174–176, 1964.; Hirt, M.L.: Use of the General Aptitude Test Battery to determine aptitude changes with age and to predict job performance. *J Appl Psychol, 43:* 36–39, 1959; Odell, C.E.: Aptitudes of work performance of the older worker. In Anderson, J.E. (Ed.): *Psychological Aspects of Aging.* Washington, D.C., American Psychological Association, 1956, pp. 240–244; Stein, C.I.: The GATB: The effect of age on intersample variations. *Personnel and Guidance Journal, 40:* 779–785, 1962; United States Department of Labor: *op cit.,* 1967, p. 223.

casions, separated by a number of years, his rate of aging relative to his group can be estimated by his ability scores as normed against the age and socioeconomic status group. A man who has abilities declining more slowly than his coevals will have a higher position relative to his age group on the second testing than would a man whose abilities are declining more rapidly with age.

Since such relative rates of aging can vary for the different abilities measured, it should be possible to identify these different patterns. For example, the man whose score on the Disassemble test at age thirty-five put him in the top 25 percent while at age fifty-five he is in the bottom 10 percent relative to his group is aging very rapidly in finger and wrist dexterity. If this same client does not drop in other test scores, for example, in Name Comparison, then specific disease processes such as atherosclerosis may be involved.

The third question: in what specific ways is the test information useful to the employment counselor?—in his office? There are three answers, and the first is that the scores provide the counselor with a way of comparing the general level of ability of appropriate clients with the level of abilities of employed age peers of different social class backgrounds. Usually it is fairly easy to estimate the SES level of particular occupations; therefore, the greatest value of the scores is that the counselor can estimate the probable success with which a person of a given age and socioeconomic status might adapt to vocational training in a range of new occupations. The data in this paper show that younger men or men from higher socioeconomic status perform better on the tests than older men or men from lower socioeconomic status. Therefore, use of the scores in this article could help prevent the counselor from overestimating the abilities of younger men or those from higher SES backgrounds or from underestimating the scores of older men or those from lower SES backgrounds.

There is a second answer to the question concerning the use of these scores. Sometimes, because of peculiarities in local employment or the newness of an occupation, the relationships between test scores and an occupation may not be known or are incorrect. However, as long as it is possible to establish the general SES level of the occupation, the aptitude requirements can be estimated.

A third value of these scores is not directly related to vocational counseling of individuals, but rather to manpower planning. When industries are planning moves into a region, it is often necessary to estimate the manpower resources required. Scores such as the present ones may be used to estimate manpower resources. If census data with age and SES distributions are available, the number of potential workers within a given range of scores on any aptitude may be estimated by reference to Tables such as these. In this way the director of employment services may help in efforts to attract industry to an area or to plan regional vocational training programs.

Basis of Scores: Sample and Testing Procedure

Sample. The subjects were 1,146 men ranging in age from twenty-eight to eighty-three years of age. All were participants in a longitudinal study of healthy aging conducted by the Boston Veterans Administration Outpatient Clinic.[3] By various medical criteria, the men were above average in health at time of entry into the study. With a few exceptions, e.g. some men over sixty years of age, all subjects were veterans.

The distribution and mean years of education of the men according to six age groups and four socioeconomic levels is given in Table 10-I.[4] The Warner occupational levels of each man were estimated on the basis of his occupation at the time of testing, or if retired, on the basis of his occupation at the time of retirement. In the Warner system, occupational level 1 is the highest occupational class and level 7 is the least skilled level. The age groupings were selected to yield a reasonable

---

3. Bell, B., Rose, C.L., and Damon, A.: The Veterans Administration longitudinal study of healthy aging. *Gerontologist, 6:* 179–184, 1966.
4. See: Warner, W.L., Meeker, M. and Eells, K.: *Social Class in America. The Evaluation of Status.* New York, Harper, 1960 for the rationale underlying the classification scheme.

TABLE 10-I
MEANS AND STANDARD DEVIATIONS OF YEARS OF EDUCATION
AND DISTRIBUTION OF SAMPLE BY AGE AND SES

Measure	25–35	36–40	41–45	46–50	51–55	56–83
			Age Group			
			Warner Levels 1–2			
Mean	15.44	15.31	15.34	15.05	14.88	15.49
SD	1.75	1.90	1.87	2.15	2.02	1.83
N	(75)	(80)	(82)	(65)	(51)	(47)
			Warner Level 3			
Mean	13.92	14.40	13.29	13.27	13.51	13.63
SD	2.29	2.20	2.50	2.14	2.44	2.72
N	(79)	(63)	(62)	(56)	(49)	(41)
			Warner Level 4			
Mean	12.10	12.53	11.76	12.22	12.86	11.72
SD	1.60	1.93	1.22	1.54	2.01	1.53
N	(39)	(55)	(67)	(41)	(28)	(18)
			Warner Levels 5–7			
Mean	11.97	12.03	12.04	11.64	11.94	10.87
SD	1.75	1.40	1.12	1.84	3.10	1.98
N	(30)	(29)	(24)	(25)	(17)	(23)

number of cases in each cell. The median age of the oldest group was fifty-nine years.

Table 10-I shows that, as expected, the average number of years of education declines with occupational level. The increase in the standard deviations of the years of education as Warner Level increases reflects both a drop from a "ceiling" of sixteen years of education as well as the grouping of Warner levels 5, 6, and 7.

Two exceptions to the overall trends indicated in Table 10-I are noteworthy. One is the depression in the mean years of education and the increase in standard deviations for Warner Levels 1–2 in age groups forty-six to fifty and fifty-one to fifty-five. The second is the elevation in years of education in Warner Level 4 in the same two age categories, accompanied by an increase in the size of the standard deviation in age category fifty-one to fifty-five. The educational level may reflect a peculiarity of the present sample; the majority of the subjects in Warner Level 4 were firemen and policemen.

Test Procedure. Form B-1002 of the Battery was used with all subjects. The standard GATB devices were used for Parts 9–12 of the test.

The Battery was administered to men, in groups ranging in size up to twenty-five by trained personnel under the direction of a qualified psychologist. Each subtest was administered in accordance with published directions for its use.[5] Most subjects received all subtests in a single session. Parts 9–12 were administered first, then parts 1–7. For about 230 men, parts 1–7 were administered in a second testing session. For all but the 230 subjects the administration of the GATB preceded the administration of an untimed personality inventory.

Meaning of Scores to Counselors. Norms are most useful when the client's background is similar to that of the members of the reference group. Some limitations of the present scores follow. The sample represents a group of men who were rigidly screened for physical health. Since the same medical standards were uniformly applied to all subjects, it means that the older subjects represent a relatively more select group.[6] Also with the exception of some subjects (mostly those over 60), all are veterans. In the younger and older age groups, the sample is necessarily less representative of the male population because relatively fewer men in these age groups are veterans. The subjects are also above average in their geographic and occupational stability.[7] Aside from the health criteria, other characteristics of the sample that should be kept in mind include the following: (a) less than 1 percent are non-Caucasian; (b) almost all live in the greater Boston area; and (c) the very lowest SES groups are poorly represented. The health restriction in the present sample allows the counselor to compare test scores of a client with those of age and SES peers who are "ideal" in the sense that their scores are not typically complicated by physical infirmities or problems associated with coincident unemployment.

5. United States Department of Labor: *Manual for the General Aptitude Test Battery.* Section F, Administration and Scoring. Washington, D.C., Government Printing Office, 1962.
6. Bell, B., Rose, C.L., and Damon, A.: *op. cit.*
7. Rose, C.L., and Bell, B.: Selection of geographically stable subjects in longitudinal studies of aging. *J Am Geriatr Soc, 12:* 143–151, 1965.

The Scores and Their Use

The data for the twelve GATB subtests will be presented first, followed by those for the nine GATB Aptitudes that are derived from them. For both, examples will be presented for using the scores. Finally, the results of some of the statistical evaluations of the data are summarized. Before presenting the norms, the Warner Level classifications should be briefly reviewed.[8] In general, Warner Levels 1 and 2 include professional and high level managerial occupations. Warner Level 3 includes many sales and proprietary, as well as technician and inspection occupations. Warner Level 4 includes policemen, firemen, postal workers, and factory foremen. Levels 5 to 7 include skilled and unskilled laborers. (The present sample included about twenty-five examples of occupations rated Warner Level 5, ten rated Warner Level 6 and one rated Warner Level 7.) Details for deriving Warner Levels are shown in the Appendix.

Subtests. The data on each of the twelve subtests are presented by means of a nomograph which allows a person's score on the test to be estimated from a knowledge of his age and SES classification. Such nomographs for the tests are presented in the twelve panels of Figure 10–1. The amount of space taken by the Age (lefthand) and SES or Warner Level (righthand) points indicate the relative strengths of the two factors in influencing the given subtest score. The predicted scores are in the middle line. The average for all men on a test is shown by the dark horizontal line. The average standard deviation for each test is shown in the lower right of each panel.

It is easy to use the nomographs. Place a straightedge between the Warner Level and Age scales. The result is a direct reading of the predicted test score in the units of the test. The standard deviation shown next to each nomograph provides a conservative measure of variability for the predicted scores. This standard deviation is the average of the observed standard deviations of the twenty-four groups of subjects on the test in question. The separation of the categories on the Age and

---

8. Warner, W.L., Meeker, M., and Eells, K.: *op. cit.*

Warner Level groupings gives a direct, visual impression of the relative importance of particular Age and SES categories in determining a test score. The horizontal line represents the mean of all the subjects on that test, and thus provides an additional way to evaluate a score in terms of the location of particular age and Warner Level groupings. Two examples follow which illustrate the use of the nomographs.

Example One. Information—Mr. Jones is a fireman aged forty-two years. His score on the Name Comparison subtest is 31. Name Comparison requires discrimination of small differences in the spelling of printed words. Interpret his score. Use of nomograph—Mr. Jones' Warner Level is 4. He is in the forty-one to forty-five year age group. Place a straightedge (preferably a clear, plastic ruler) over the dot representing the forty-one to forty-five year age group on the left, and the 4 in the right hand column. The predicted score is about 43. We note that Mr. Jones' score of 31 is substantially below the expected value for his age and SES level, as well as that of the "average man." He is about one standard deviation below his own peers' expected score which means that some 85 percent of the scores for his group lie above his. Since Warner Level is an important indicator of performance of this test, one would check to see if Mr. Jones' education is less than that expected for his group.

Example Two. Information—Mr. Smith is a shop salesman, fifty-five years of age, who obtained a score of 32 on the Disassemble subtest. The test requires the removal of rivets and washers from a pegboard. Mr. Smith's Warner Level is estimated to be 3, and he is between fifty-one and fifty-five years of age. Use of nomograph—place the rule over the dot numbered 3 on the Warner Level scale, and the dot for the fifty-one to fifty-five year group. Note that Warner Level 3 is a bit lower than Warner Level 4. Mr. Smith's expected score is about 25. Note that Warner Level effects are very small, a characteristic that is in contrast to the previous example. For a man of Mr. Smith's age differences in Warner Level would change the expected scores by about four points, at most. The striking thing about Mr. Smith's score is that it is closer to

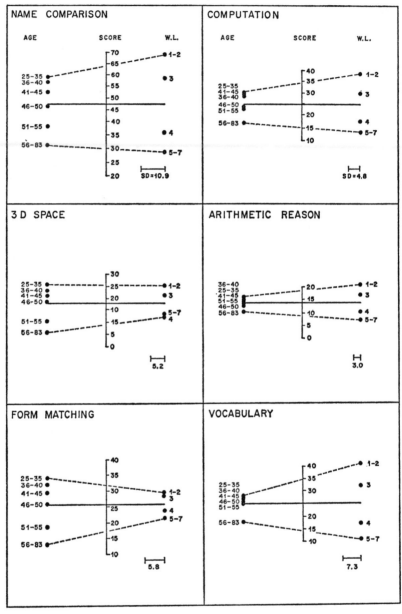

Figure 10–1. Twelve nomographs from which expected scores on twelve GATB subtests (middle line of each panel) may be predicted from four Warner Level (W.L. right vertical line) and six age (left vertical line)

≫

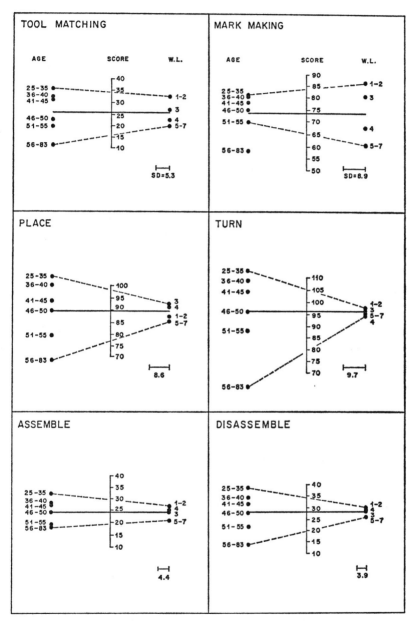

categories. The horizontal line in each panel represents the grand mean for all groups for that test. Standard deviations (SD) shown are average standard deviations for 24 groups (lower right of each panel).

that of a man fifteen to twenty years his junior. It is two standard deviations higher than that of his own age group, so that only some 2 or 3 percent of the men in his age group would be expected to have higher scores. Since scores on the Disassemble Test are relatively independent of occupational history, we would expect Mr. Smith to do well on tasks which require fine finger movements regardless of his competition.

In summary, the nomographs are useful for counseling purposes, because they show a client's score in relation to both the mean of all the subjects as well as to any particular combination of age and SES. With the present data, they technically represent the best predictions of ability scores available from linear combinations of age and SES classifications. The nomographs are simple to use and allow for interpolation between the given SES or age groups.

Factors Underlying the Structure of the Nomographs. Inspection of the nomographs shows that performance on some tests is controlled mostly by SES differences: Arithmetic Reason, Vocabulary, and Computation are the best examples. In contrast, others (e.g. Disassemble as shown in the second example), are influenced almost entirely by differences in age.

The degree to which performance on each test is influenced by differences in age and SES was assessed with statistical analyses. First, multivariate analysis of variance was performed with Age and SES as the two factors and the scores of the twelve GATB subtests as the dependent variables.[9] Results of the analysis reported by Nuttall and Fozard showed that the main effects for Age and SES, but not their interaction, were significant.

Results of univariate analyses of variance performed on the twelve tests separately also showed that in none of the tests was there a significant interaction between Age and SES. However, there were significant effects of Age and SES on the twelve tests. All twelve tests had significant Age effects; nine tests showed significant SES effects. Place, Turn, and Disassemble were not significantly related to SES.

9. Nuttall, R.L., and Fozard, J.L.: Age, socioeconomic status and human abilities. *Aging and Human Development, 1:* 164, 1967.

The percentage of variance accounted for by the main effects of Age and SES were computed for each subtest, and the results are shown in Figure 10–2. In general, Figure 10–2 shows that those tests most influenced by Age were least influenced by SES and vice versa. Only two tests, 3D Space and Mark Making, seemed to be nearly equally influenced by both variables. As indicated in Figure 10–2, some subtests which contribute to the same aptitude score are affected differently by age and SES, notably Assemble and Disassemble (Aptitude F) and 3D Space, Arithmetic Reason, and Vocabulary (Aptitude G).

Aptitude scores. The means and standard deviations for the nine GATB aptitude scores for each of the twenty-four classifications by age and SES are presented in Table 10-II. The letter after each aptitude name in Table 10-II is the standard abbreviated name of the aptitude.

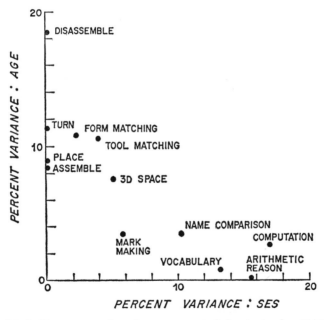

Figure 10–2. Percentage of variance accounted for in twelve GATB subtests by differences in four Warner Level (SES) and six age classifications. Percentages of variance were calculated assuming a fixed factor analysis of variance.

TABLE 10-II
MEANS* AND STANDARD DEVIATIONS† OF GATB APTITUDES
BY AGE AND OCCUPATION

Warner Level	Age Group					
	25–35	36–40	41–45	46–50	51–55	56–83
	G—Intelligence					
1–2	125.9	123.9	123.3	120.6	118.0	111.9
	14.1	17.3	15.2	14.2	16.1	15.1
3	118.2	119.3	115.8	115.3	111.4	109.1
	16.7	13.7	14.0	14.5	15.5	18.6
4	107.5	108.5	104.8	105.2	108.1	99.4
	15.0	15.1	14.3	16.3	15.2	20.1
5–7	104.4	102.8	105.2	101.8	100.7	98.0
	16.0	14.6	14.2	13.7	16.1	12.0
	V—Verbal Aptitude					
1–2	121.5	120.8	120.8	116.0	116.2	112.7
	14.3	17.1	15.7	15.1	15.2	16.5
3	116.6	115.2	112.3	114.5	111.6	109.8
	16.9	14.1	13.5	14.6	16.4	16.1
4	104.2	107.2	104.6	107.4	110.9	100.1
	13.4	14.3	12.2	16.6	11.9	19.4
5–7	102.5	101.3	104.3	103.4	101.8	102.6
	15.4	14.5	12.7	12.8	15.4	13.8
	N—Numerical Aptitude					
1–2	126.4	122.2	123.2	120.3	117.6	114.9
	15.4	16.1	16.1	15.0	16.1	16.1
3	118.5	118.7	115.7	112.6	110.9	108.5
	16.3	15.5	16.0	19.1	16.2	20.2
4	104.9	106.5	105.0	103.8	108.5	98.1
	14.6	14.3	13.4	16.4	18.4	18.8
5–7	102.8	102.5	104.3	98.2	99.2	94.7
	16.0	14.3	12.8	13.2	15.3	14.1
	S—Spatial Aptitude					
1–2	114.6	113.7	111.3	107.9	105.2	96.3
	17.2	18.9	16.4	16.3	16.2	14.4
3	108.7	110.8	109.6	107.5	98.0	96.2
	17.1	17.5	15.3	14.9	15.2	15.9
4	105.7	105.5	98.5	99.2	93.3	90.8
	14.5	18.1	18.1	16.4	15.1	18.5
5–7	106.3	99.2	103.9	100.6	94.2	91.3
	15.1	15.7	14.1	15.6	16.9	13.3
	P—Form Perception					
1–2	117.7	115.5	113.4	105.6	100.5	91.8
	15.5	17.6	18.0	15.4	16.0	16.4
3	112.7	109.8	107.1	104.3	97.7	90.3
	19.0	20.0	19.3	19.8	19.1	16.9
4	107.8	109.4	101.0	94.7	96.5	87.8
	18.0	16.9	16.3	17.5	12.9	23.0
5–7	104.5	98.7	104.0	96.6	89.8	87.8
	20.7	14.1	16.2	15.7	13.9	18.7
	Q—Clerical Perception					
1–2	124.9	125.8	124.5	120.1	118.8	115.8
	16.2	16.1	15.2	16.0	15.7	13.8
3	123.8	123.6	117.4	118.6	113.7	113.4

TABLE 10-II (cont'd)

Warner Level	Age Group					
	25–35	36–40	41–45	46–50	51–55	56–83
	17.9	16.8	15.4	16.9	15.7	14.1
4	114.4	114.8	109.3	113.1	109.7	103.9
	13.8	12.7	12.3	15.4	17.0	18.5
5–7	110.9	108.1	114.5	106.2	105.4	103.3
	16.8	13.1	13.1	12.8	13.0	13.1
K—Motor Coordination						
1–2	118.2	117.8	112.8	115.2	111.3	107.8
	14.7	17.8	16.6	16.9	17.6	20.5
3	117.9	116.6	111.9	113.0	108.5	100.5
	18.5	16.2	16.7	21.4	15.4	19.5
4	105.6	106.4	107.5	107.2	105.1	98.2
	18.5	16.3	18.4	15.4	20.6	22.1
5–7	104.9	104.0	107.7	100.1	98.8	95.2
	19.9	13.0	12.7	12.7	16.8	17.5
F—Finger Dexterity						
1–2	98.8	89.3	89.6	85.6	77.1	70.9
	20.7	17.8	19.4	18.9	19.0	20.0
3	92.9	91.2	86.0	83.4	76.7	65.5
	21.0	19.0	20.3	20.3	20.7	23.1
4	95.6	89.8	86.8	79.5	75.8	73.5
	16.6	16.1	17.3	17.4	19.9	24.8
5–7	87.5	85.1	86.2	81.0	70.0	62.3
	16.8	18.2	18.1	18.8	13.0	19.0
M—Manual Dexterity						
1–2	107.2	102.5	98.4	93.6	92.4	80.1
	23.1	18.4	19.5	17.0	18.9	18.4
3	104.8	108.3	99.2	97.6	96.4	82.4
	20.1	20.1	21.8	22.0	20.1	19.2
4	106.3	103.5	99.9	94.8	88.3	89.3
	20.3	17.3	17.3	20.9	22.8	22.8
5–7	103.9	98.9	101.3	99.6	86.2	76.4
	19.9	18.4	15.7	17.0	15.7	25.4

* Top number in each cell is the mean.
† Bottom number in each cell is standard deviation.

Table 10-II shows that with respect to the mean of one hundred and the standard deviation of twenty to which all of the aptitude scores are scaled, the averages of all of the present groups are high except for Aptitudes F and M. The high values of the means on aptitudes which are most susceptible to SES differences reflect the fact that 69 percent of the subjects in Warner Levels 5 to 7 are actually from Level 5. Warner Levels 6 and 7 are 21 percent and 10 percent of the group, respectively, in the present study.

Use of the Tables is similar to that for the nomographs. Note the age of the client and estimate the Warner Level for his occupation. Then enter Table 10-II to find the expected scores for his age group on the nine Aptitudes. In each case, two standards for comparison of the scores of a client are possible. One is with the client's own employed peers as indicated in Table 10-II. The second is with the Labor Department norms which need no Tables because the mean and standard deviation for all of them are the same, i.e. 100 and 20, respectively.

Example Three. Information—Mr. Brown is an electrician who is fifty-five years-old. His calculated score on Aptitude M, Manual Dexterity, is 130. Evaluate his performance. Use of Tables—The Warner Level for electrician is 5 and the reference age group is fifty-one to fifty-five years. The expected mean is 86.2 and the standard deviation is 15.7. Mr. Brown's score is well above average for his age, over two standard deviations. This means that we would expect less than 2 percent of the working population to have a score higher than that of Mr. Brown. This estimate of Mr. Brown's standing is even higher than would have been found if it were compared with the GATB reference norms, because the present norms take Mr. Brown's age into account. However, in this case we see that by either standard he would qualify for any OAP in which a score for Aptitude M is employed.

Basis for Table 10-II. Nine two-way analyses of variance were conducted on the aptitudes with age and SES as factors. The unweighted cell means procedure was employed for each. Results of the analyses showed statistically significant age effects for all aptitudes. Aptitude V was significant at the 0.05 level, the others were significant at the 0.001 level. In all cases, mean scores declined with age. The effect of SES was statistically significant for eight of the nine aptitudes. Aptitude M did not change significantly with SES. Aptitude F was significant only at the 0.01 level. All seven of the other aptitudes declined with SES level significantly at the 0.001 level. For none of the nine aptitudes was there a significant interaction between Age and SES. Details of these analyses are described elsewhere.[10]

10. Fozard, J.L., and Nuttall, R.L.: General Aptitude Test Battery Score for men differing in age and socioeconomic status. *J Appl Psychol,* 55: 372–379, 1971.

The percentage of variance accounted for by the main effects of Age and SES in the nine analyses of variance were computed, based on the procedure described by Hays.[11] The results are shown in Figure 10–3. The percentage accounted for by SES in each aptitude is on the horizontal axis, that for Age on the vertical axis.

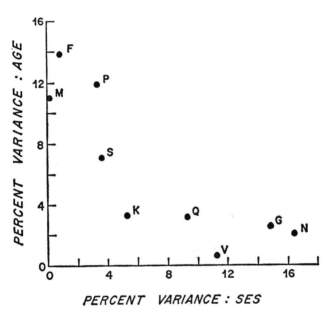

Figure 10–3. Percentage of variance accounted for in nine GATB Aptitudes by differences in four Warner Level (SES) and six age classifications. Percentages of variance were calculated assuming a fixed factor analysis of variance.

The magnitudes of the values in Figure 10–3 reflect the fact that differences in SES influence the Aptitudes N, G, V, and Q most. On the other hand, Aptitudes F, P, and M were most affected by Age. In contrast to the results of the "Four State" Study the effect of Age on Aptitude V was statistically significant in the present study.[12] Note that in the aptitudes most influenced by SES differences, for example, Aptitudes G, N, and

11. Hays, W.L.: *Statistics for Psychologists*. New York, Holt, Rinehart, and Winston, 1963.
12. United States Department of Labor: *op. cit.*, 1967, p. 225.

V, there is a tendency for differences between Warner Levels 1 to 2 and 5 to 7 to be smaller with older age groups than with younger ones. In the case of Aptitudes G and V, this trend was statistically significant. The results of all the analyses of the present data show unequivocally that there is no statistically significant interaction between the main effects of Age and SES. Thus, there is no evidence in the present data to support the idea that age decrements in cognitive functioning decline less in high than in low SES groups.[13]

Application of the procedure for assessing differential declines in extreme SES groups to the GATB Aptitude data showed that the amount of decline in Aptitudes G and V was different for Warner Levels 1 to 2 and 5 to 7. However, in contrast to Heron and Chown's results which showed the largest difference between the two SES groups at the oldest ages, the differences in Aptitudes G and N are smallest in the oldest age groups. Even allowing for differences in tests and systems of SES classifications in two samples, it would not be expected that the age trends would be directly opposite, particularly in Aptitude G which is the best unitary measure of general intelligence in the GATB.[14] One explanation of the discrepancy is that educational differences in SES in the British sample were greater in the older than in the younger groups. Alternatively, one could argue that the lowest SES groups were not well represented in the present group, particularly in the oldest age groups. As a result, the observed age differences in those groups are not as large as in the general population. Possibly, the differential age effect in high and low SES groups observed by Heron and Chown is peculiar to the Progressive Matrices Test. In any case, the effects of SES on age differences of aptitudes in the present study provide an additional pattern to the ones described by Botwinick in his review of age differences in patterns of ability.[15]

---

13. Heron and Chown, S.: *Age and Function.* Boston, Little Brown, 1967.
14. United States Department of Labor: *op. cit.,* 1967, Ch. 14.
15. Botwinick, J.: *Cognitive Processes in Maturity and Old Age.* New York. Springer, 1967, p. 24.

Conclusions and Implications

The major trends of the nomographs (Fig. 10-1) and Table 10-II may be summarized as follows: (a) Age and SES affect average performance on the GATB aptitudes, as well as the twelve GATB subtests on which the aptitudes are based, (b) there were no statistically significant interactions between the effects of Age and SES when all Warner Levels were considered. However, when the data of only the two extreme SES groups were used, in GATB Aptitudes G and V there was a statistically significant tendency for differences in the abilities of high and low SES groups to become *smaller* with age, (c) in general, scores which were most influenced by Age were least influenced by SES and vice versa.

The most immediate, practical implication of the present data for counseling is for the interpretation of Aptitude Scores with reference to the Occupational Aptitude Patterns. Considerable caution and judgment must be exercised by the counselor in applying the OAP cutting scores to older workers. The possibility exists that some scores of older workers may be too low.

The problem may be illustrated with the data of Table 10-II. The average scores on the Aptitudes for each of the twenty-four groups in Table 10-II was compared to the cut-off scores for each of the thirty-six OAPs.[16] The percentage of OAPs which were "passed" by these mean scores are indicated in Figure 10-4. Clear differences are observed between the SES levels, especially between Warner Levels 1 to 2 and 3, as contrasted to Warner Levels 4 and 5 to 7. However, Age seemed to have a stronger effect than SES, with all four SES groups dropping precipitously with advancing age. The highest SES group qualified for all thirty-six OAP's when young but when old they qualified for only seventeen OAPs. Similarly, the lowest SES group qualified for twenty-eight OAPs on the basis of their average scores at the youngest age, but only for nine OAPs at the oldest age. Clearly, the older worker in all SES groups is severely handicapped when compared with younger

---

16. United States Department of Labor: *op. cit.,* 1962.

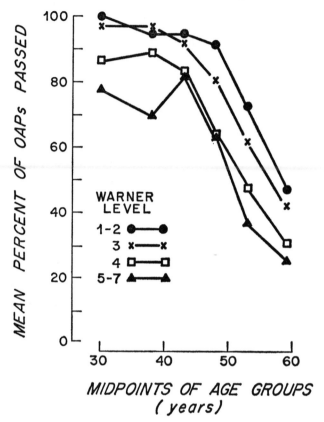

Figure 10–4. Percentage of thirty-six Occupational Pattern Structures (OAP's) passed by average of men in each of the combinations of age and SES.

men on the basis of present OAP cut-off scores. Note that some of these declines occur within the eighteen to fifty-four year age range covered by the GATB standardization group.

The present data suggest no concrete procedures for "adjusting" OAP scores. However, the counselor may judiciously use the norms to supplement his judgments on the trainability of clients.

As an example, suppose the counselor has a client whose present occupational level is low in relationship to his abilities on the tests that are most influenced by differences in SES. This client may well be a "good bet" for training for other oc-

cupations which require verbal and numerical abilities as well
as other occupations within his present SES level for which he
qualifies by experience. On the other hand, consideration of
the training possibilities for a client with respect to occupations
which demand a high degree of psychomotor ability should
be more conservative.

One may argue that there should be no adjustments in OAPs
for older workers because an individual, young or old, needs
the same abilities to succeed in a particular family of occupations for which a SAP (Specific Aptitude Pattern) or OAP
is applicable. However, such reasoning assumes, *a priori,* that
the establishment of OAPs was done in a manner that is equally
valid for younger and older workers, and convincing empirical
support for such a viewpoint is not available.

In any case, until the relationship between age differences in
GATB scores and OAPs is clarified, the GATB can be used
profitably in vocational counseling of older workers if it is considered as a tool for assessment of human abilities that describes
an individual's potential relative to his age and social class peers.

APPENDIX

The measure of socioeconomic status (SES) employed was
adapted from Warner, Meeker and Eells.[17] The Warner measure is a two-way classification of seven types and seven levels
of occupations. The job type categories are based upon a rather
standard grouping of occupations according to the kind of
work entailed in a given occupation, e.g. Professionals, Business Men, Manual Workers, etc. The occupational level scale
which was the measure employed in the present study was
originally devised on the basis of income and prestige ratings
accorded to a particular occupation. An important characteristic of the job level measure is that it cuts across the job type
classification, e.g. lawyers, in the Professional category, and
Certified Public Accountants, in the Clerical category, are both
assigned a rating of *one* on the job level dimension. The possible job level assigned to a particular type of occupation is

17. Warner, W.L., Meeker, M.; Eells, K.: *op. cit.,* pp. 140–141.

not the same for all seven job types. For example, all Professional occupations are rated 1, 2, or 3 on job level, whereas Protective and Service Worker occupations are rated only 4 through 7.

Following are examples of occupations which are represented in the present sample in the seven Warner Level categories. Warner Level 1 is assigned to such occupations as, physician, engineer, lawyer, college professor, executives of banking and insurance, and certified public accountants.

Some examples of Warner Level 2 rated occupations are: high school teacher, school principal, rehabilitation counselor, bank, office, insurance and sales managers; accountant; programmer, and farmer.

Occupations for Warner Level 3 are: draftsman, surveyor, elementary school teacher, proprietor, underwriter, government investigator, postal clerk, and computer operator.

Warner Level 4 includes: store manager, bookkeeper, office clerk, factory foreman, police, fireman, and barber.

Warner Level 5: painter, carpenter, machinist, repairman, vehicle driver, gas station attendant, restaurant worker, and bartender.

Occupations falling in the last two Warner Level categories are: for Warner Level 6, semiskilled factory worker, stock worker, guard, hospital attendant, and custodian; and for Warner Level 7, unskilled laborer.

V. AGE AND CAPACITY

Chapter 11

AGE AND CAPACITY DEVALUATION

LAWRENCE D. HABER

The patterns of labor force and social withdrawal associated with aging are predicated on the assumption of declining capacities with age. There is general agreement that as people get older, they tend to lose many of their adult roles and functions. The role responsibilities of the family life cycle are largely scheduled by normative expectations about the appropriate ages for marriage and childbearing. Age and seniority constraints institutionalize occupational choices and role changes in hiring, promotion and retirement practices. These social expectations reflect, to some extent, expectations about biological changes associated with aging.

This paper is concerned with the relationship of aging to disability and their effect on employment and social activity in the working age population. The relationship of aging to health impairments and capacity losses is well known and has been extensively documented. Performance requirements are affected by age through the operation of personnel practices, seniority systems and technological change. There is also reason to believe that social expectations about age and aging affect the capacities and perception of capacities of older people.

The biological decrements of the aging process are usually gradual and often become marked only late in life.[1] Physical

Note: Reprinted from the *J Health Soc Behav*, No. 11, September, 1970.

The interpretations and conclusions expressed in this paper are the author's and are not intended to represent the position or policy of the Social Security Administration.

1. Welford, A.T.: Industrial work suitable for older people: Some British studies. *Gerontologist*, 6: 4–9 March, 1966. Birren, James E.: *Handbook of Aging and the Individuals: Psychological and Biological Aspects*. Chicago, University of Chicago Press, 1959. Botwinick, Jack: *Cognitive Processes in Maturity and Old-Age*, New York, Springer, 1967. Breen, Leonard Z.: The Aging Individual. In Tibbitts, Clark (Ed.): *Handbook of Social Gerontology*. Chicago, University of Chicago Press, 1960, pp. 145–164.

capacities start to decline during the twenties. Environmental stress, chronic diseases and cellular maturation reduce the physiological capacity for maintenance and regeneration; progressive physical degeneration results in the loss or reduction of sensory acuity, physical coordination, muscular strength, and endurance. Reaction time slows down and cognitive abilities, memory and perception tend to decline.

The clinical significance of many physiological changes is unknown. Socially, capacity changes are significant only in relation to their effect on the behavior or the expectations of individuals. Capacity losses which limit the ability of the individual to meet performance expectations may result in a state of disability, in which the incapacity of the individual is recognized and behavioral alternatives or role modifications are permitted. The circumstances under which an impairment is recognized as disabling, however, vary greatly with the capacities of the individual and situational requirements. The residual capacities of the individual may influence the extent and severity of disability, as compensating capabilities. The flexibility of the role requirements, the availability of alternative role occupants and the willingness of reciprocal role members to accept modifications in performance requirements also mediate the severity of the disability.

Employment practices and social attitudes suggest that the association of aging and capacity declines has produced generalized expectations about the capacities of older people. Performance or potential for performance may be evaluated in terms of the "diffuse status characteristics"[2] assigned to middle or old-age, regardless of the relationship of task requirements to age limitations or the limitations of a given individual. The association of aging with capacity loss leads to the identification of chronological age as, in itself, a measure of capacity.

Arbitrary age limits on hiring and employer preference for younger workers, for example, are usually attributed to physical capability requirements.[3] These age restrictions, however

2. Berger, Joseph, Zelditch, Jr., M. and Anderson, B.: *Sociological Theories in Progress.* Boston, Houghton Mifflin, 1966, vol. 1, pp. 32–45.
3. U.S. Department of Labor: *The Older American Worker: Age Dis*

appear to be more affected by labor supply conditions than by the physical requirements of the job. Factory production decreases only slightly between age forty-five to sixty. Industrial studies indicate that the effect of ability deterioration on occupational skills is relatively slight before age sixty.[4]

The older worker is often identified as inflexible, untrainable or uninsurable on the basis of age or actuarial estimates alone. His own socialization towards aging and confrontation with the attitudes and behavior of employers tend to confirm these expectations and may lead to a lower evaluation of his capacities than for a younger man with comparable skills or impairments.

Older workers, for example, are more reluctant to seek retraining and more readily accept occupational downgrading than young workers. Belbin and Belbin point out that age is a significant factor in evaluating a worker's adaptability to the demands of a new situation.[5] Although there is some physical basis for losses in adaptability and trainability, flexibility is also diminished by lack of practice in adapting and modifying behavior. The relative stability of the environment of older people probably provides less practice in adaptation.

Technological change and industrial composition also contribute to the devaluation of the skills of older people. Older workers tend to be more concentrated than young workers in declining and static industries, in which low growth rates and high unemployment levels prejudice the transferability of skills.[6]

----

crimination in Employment. Report of the Secretary of Labor to the Congress. Washington, D.C., Government Printing Office, 1965, pp. 17–28.

4. Welford, A.T.: *Aging and Human Skill.* London, Oxford University Press, 1958.

5. Belbin, E., and Belbin, R.M.: New careers in middle age. In Neugarten, Bernice L. (Ed.): *Middle Age and Aging.* Chicago, University of Chicago Press, 1968, pp. 341–346.

6. Jaffe, A.J.: Technology, opportunity and the older worker. In *Employment of the Middle-Aged Worker.* New York, National Council on the Aging, 1969, pp. 281–341. Schupack, M.B.: Research on employment problems of older workers. *Gerontologist, 2:* 157–163, March, 1962.

The importance of age as a barrier to employment and job mobility of displaced workers has been noted in many studies.[7]

There are few exemptions from work involvement for men in the working ages, other than incapacity. Unexcused withdrawal exposes the individual to sanctions for deviant behavior, including separation from economic rewards.[8] For most men, work is their only major economic resource. Early departure from the labor force cuts off their primary source of income and separates them from a basic source of social identification, meaningful activity and peer group associations.[9]

After adjustment to entry into the labor market, men are expected to work until an orderly and normatively acceptable time of retirement.[10] Even those for whom work is not an economic necessity are expected to demonstrate an appropriate orientation to achievement.[11]

After age sixty-five, retirement provides an alternative social context for the aged worker and alternative means of support. Institutional structures and practices, however, rigorously separate behavioral expectations for men before and after age sixty-five. Although early retirement is available to men at age sixty-two, the economic inducements are smaller and there is little compulsion. Underemployment, unemployment and re-

7. Aiken, Michael, Ferman, Louis A., and Sheppard, Harold L.: *Economic Failure, Alienation and Extremism.* Ann Arbor, University of Michigan Press, 1968, pp. 31 and 48–49. Wilcock, Richard C., and Franke, Walter H.: *Unwanted Workers.* New York, Free Press, 1953.

8. Cohen, Albert K.: The study of social disorganization and deviant behavior. In Merton, Robert K. *et al.* (Eds.): *Sociology Today.* New York, Basic Books, 1959, pp. 470–472.

9. Friedmann, E.A., and Havighurst, R.J.: Work and retirement. In Nosow, S., and Form, W.H. (Eds.): *Man, Work and Society.* New York, Basic Books, 1962, pp. 41–55. Morse, Nancy C., and Weiss R.S.: The function and meaning of work and the job. *Am Sociol Rev. 20:* 191–198, April, 1955.

10. Barfield, Richard, and Morgan, James: *Early Retirement.* Ann Arbor, Institute for Social Research, 1969, pp. 11 and 54–55. Slavick, Fred: *Compulsory and Flexible Retirement in the American Economy.* Ithaca, Cornell University, 1966, p. 18.

11. Morse and Weiss, *op. cit.*

employment problems, however, frequently start in the forties and fifties, when family requirements are still relatively high and retirement is neither an available nor a feasible alternative. Labor force participation and income tend to decline after age forty-five, while the incidence of poverty and of extended unemployment increase.[12]

Although normatively and institutionally devalued, advancing age provides few exemptions from role requirements before retirement. The acceptance of disability, however, excuses the individual from responsibility for his performance limitations, as a condition beyond his control and permits modification of role expectations in terms of devalued capacities.[13]

The severity and prevalence of disability may, therefore, be affected by social definitions of aging, independently of the capacity limitations and performance requirements associated with aging. To the extent that aging in itself is a significant factor in capacity devaluation, older people should have less ability to cope with the effects of functional losses and to meet occupational requirements than younger people. Older workers will be more severely disabled by capacity losses than younger workers; the relationship between age and disability should therefore persist when capacity limitations and capacity requirements are taken into account.

STUDY METHOD

The data are based on a national survey conducted by the Social Security Administration in 1966; a multiframe area probability sample was selected to represent the noninstitutionalized civilian population aged eighteen to sixty-four of the United States. The survey was conducted in two stages: first, all

12. Ravin, L.H.: Testimony on problems in the implementation of the older worker program. *Hearings of the Special Committee on Aging, U.S. Senate, 90th Congress, Adequacy of Service for Older Workers,* Part I. Washington, D.C., U.S. Government Printing Office, 1968, pp. 175–183.
13. Haber, Lawrence D., and Smith, Richard T.: Disability and deviance: Normative adaptations in role behavior. *Am Sociol Rev. 36:* 87–97, Feb., 1971.

sample households were screened to identify people aged eighteen to sixty-four with health-related limitations in their ability to work;[14] personal interviews were then conducted with the adults identified as disabled to verify the disability statement and to collect data on the nature of the disability, work experience, medical care, income, demographic characteristics and other attributes of disabled persons. The Bureau of the Census was responsible for data collection and processing.

Approximately thirty thousand households were selected from seven population frames in 243 primary sampling areas. The sampling frames included households from the Census Bureau's Monthly Labor Survey and Current Population Survey, Old-age, Survivors, Disability and Health Insurance (OASDHI) disability beneficiaries, disabled recipients of public assistance and denied applicants for OASDHI disability benefits. Sample cases were weighted in proportion to their combined probability of selection and inflated to benchmark estimates of the total United States civilian noninstitutionalized population aged eighteen to sixty-four.

The disability identification questionnaires were mailed out during February-March, 1966. After two mail follow-ups, nonrespondents were contacted by personal interview callbacks. Interviews were completed with approximately 8,700 disabled adults during April to May 1966.

Disability was defined in this study as a limitation in the kind or amount of work lasting more than six months which had resulted from a chronic health condition or impairment.[15]

---

14. Haber, Lawrence D.: Identifying the disabled: Concepts and methods in the measurement of disability. *Social Security Bulletin, 30:* 17–34, Dec. 1967.

15. Haber, Lawrence D.: Disability, work and income maintenance: Prevalence of disability, 1966. *Social Security Bulletin, 30:* 14–23, May, 1968. There was a high degree of agreement in the identification of the disabled between the mail questionnaire and the follow-up interview; 95 percent of the respondents reported as disabled in the mail questionnaire were also reported as disabled in the follow-up interview. Of those who reported a health-related work limitation both times, about 5 percent changed the designation of the extent of limitation; limitation changes were dis-

The disability classification is based on the extent of the individual's capacity for work as reported by the respondent in a set of work-qualification questions: *severely disabled*—unable to work altogether or unable to work regularly; *occupationally disabled*—able to work regularly, but unable to do the same work as before the onset of disability or unable to work full time; *secondary work limitations*—able to work full time, regularly and at the same work, but with limitations in the kind or amount of work they can perform.

Major Disabling Condition. A description of the condition considered the main reason for the respondent's work limitation was obtained in the interview. Only one condition was accepted as the major disabling condition; multiple diagnoses were reclassified to designate the major disabling condition, according to an arbitrary classificatory scheme.[16]

Functional Limitations. A measure of functional impairment was developed from a set of items on limitations in performing specific physical activities and the assistance needed for physical mobility and personal care. The physical activities included lifting or carrying weights, stooping, kneeling or crouching, using stairs or inclines, walking, reaching, and handling and fingering. Mobility limitations included help needed to go outside the home or to use transportation and confinement to home or bed. Personal care limitations included help needed for dressing, eating and personal hygiene. Functional limita-

---

tributed between those reporting greater limitation and those reporting less limitation than at the initial screening. Respondents who reported that they had no work limitations or had recovered were reclassified as not disabled.

16. In almost all cases a single condition from the listing was reported. The respondent was also asked if he had talked to a doctor about it: 95 percent of the respondents had talked to a physician; three-fourths reported that the physician had used the same description. Of those reporting a different diagnosis or description, four-fifths reported a diagnosis in the same major diagnosis group as the condition originally reported. Language differences between the questionnaire, designed for lay interpretation, and the more technical terminology of the physician probably account for most of the reporting differences.

tions were classified into five groups, ranging from those with no limitations, to the functionally dependent, who needed help in mobility or personal care.

Social participation measures were based on the number of activities and tasks the respondent "now does." *Household participation* was scored from 0 to 4; task areas included shopping, heavy chores (such as heavy cleaning, care of household equipment or yard), light chores (such as cooking, sweeping and minor repairs) and money management. *Social activity* included activities in the home (inviting friends for dinner or parties) and outside the home (family outings, visits, church and clubs) and was scored as neither, one or both.

The data on labor force participation refer to employment, in the week prior to interview. Hospitalization refers to services used during the past calendar year. Work at onset of disability refers to the job held during the year that health conditions first started to limit the kind or amount of work performed.

DISABILITY PREVALENCE
AND LABOR FORCE PARTICIPATION

For a sizeable proportion of the population, social, psychological and physical effects of impairment begin long before the expected age of retirement and result in work limiting disabilities of varying degrees of severity. About one-sixth of the noninstitutionalized population of working age was disabled in 1966 (Table 11-I). The proportion disabled increased with age, from 8 percent of the youngest group, aged eighteen to thirty-four, to 36 percent of those aged fifty-five to sixty-four. The rate of disability appeared to increase at an increasing rate with each succeeding decade; prevalence was twice as high among those thirty-four to forty-four as among adults eighteen to thirty-four, three times as high among those forty-five to fifty-four, and five times as high among the population aged fifty-five to sixty-four.

Age was also directly related to the severity of disability; the sharpest distinctions between age groups were in the proportions severely disabled. Between age eighteen to thirty-four and thirty-five to forty-four, the prevalence of severe disabil-

TABLE 11-I

SEVERITY OF DISABILITY: PERCENTAGE DISTRIBUTION OF THE NONINSTITUTIONAL POPULATION
AGED 18–64 BY AGE AND SEX, 1966

Age	Total U.S. Population Aged 18–64	Non-disabled	Disabled			
	(000's)		*Total Disabled*	*Severe*	*Occupational*	*Secondary Work Limitation*
			Percentage Distribution			
TOTAL GROUP						
Total	103,085	82.8	17.2	5.9	4.9	6.4
18–34	40,574	92.2	7.8	1.7	1.8	4.3
35–44	23,693	85.7	14.3	4.7	4.0	5.6
45–54	21,896	76.8	23.2	6.9	8.2	8.1
55–64	16,922	63.8	36.2	16.4	9.1	10.7
MEN						
Total	48,980	82.8	17.2	4.7	4.9	7.6
18–34	18,977	91.7	8.3	1.4	1.8	5.1
35–44	11,370	86.9	13.1	2.8	4.5	5.8
45–54	10,567	76.8	23.2	5.3	8.4	9.6
55–64	8,066	63.9	36.1	14.4	8.3	13.4
WOMEN						
Total	54,105	82.8	17.2	7.0	4.8	5.4
18–34	21,597	92.6	7.4	2.1	1.8	3.5
35–44	12,323	84.6	15.4	6.4	3.6	5.5
45–54	11,329	76.9	23.1	8.4	7.9	6.7
55–64	8,856	63.8	36.2	18.2	9.7	8.2

ity roughly doubled; at age forty-five to fifty-four the rate of severe disability was approximately four times and at age fifty-five to sixty-four ten times that of the youngest age group. By comparison, the rate of occupational disability increased about five times over the age span and the rate of secondary disability increased less than three times.

As defined in this study, disability was directly related to limitations in work ability. Disability had a major effect on labor force participation and employment. Severe disability reduced labor force participation sharply. Occupational disability affected the level of full-time employment, but did not reduce labor force participation below that of the nondisabled; there was little difference in the level of full-time employment between the nondisabled and adults with secondary work limits.

The effect of disability on labor force participation also increased with age. Among the nondisabled men, the proportion not in the labor force was relatively low after age forty-five (Table 11-II). The proportion of the disabled who were not in the labor force, however, increased with age and the proportion employed full time decreased. With the exception of occupationally disabled men, the same pattern of reduced work involvement was found for men and women by extent of disability. By age fifty-five to sixty-four, two-fifths of the disabled men were no longer in the labor force and less than half were employed full-time.

It is apparent that the increasing effect of disability with age accounts for the decline in labor force activity among older workers under age sixty-five.[17] Severe disability affected

---

17. Disability rates increase at age sixty-two to sixty-four, when early retirement benefits become generally available and labor force participation declines. The prevalence and severity of disability at age sixty-two to sixty-four is, however, almost identical with that of men aged sixty to sixty-one, relatively few of whom had access to early retirement income. It would appear that disability stimulates early retirement; there is no indication that the availability of early retirement benefits affected the prevalence of disability or the severity of disability. See Haber, Lawrence D.: The effect of age and disability on access to public income-maintenance programs. *Social Security Survey of the Disabled.* Report Number 3. Washington, D.C., Social Security Administration, July 1968.

TABLE 11-II
LABOR FORCE PARTICIPATION

Age	U.S. Population	Non-disabled	Disabled			
			Total Disabled	Severe	Occupational	Secondary Work Limitation
Percent Not in the Labor Force						
Total Men 18–64	9.5	6.0	26.3	73.3	4.9	11.2
18–44	9.4	8.6	18.7	67.3	8.8	6.6
45–54	5.0	0.5	20.1	72.6	2.0	7.1
55–64	15.6*	2.1	39.5*	76.6*	3.7	21.8*
Total Women 18–64	54.6	51.9	67.4	85.3	62.8	48.1
18–44	55.4	55.3	60.4	80.3	57.8	44.5
45–54	48.9	44.5	63.6	81.6	60.4	44.7
55–64	58.7*	47.8	78.0*	91.3*	70.3*	57.8*
Percent Currently Employed Full Time						
Total Men 18–64	79.2	83.7	57.7	4.1	72.3	81.5
18–44	78.1	79.1	64.8	5.1	74.0	81.3
45–54	85.5	91.9	64.5	7.0	71.7	89.9
55–64	75.1*	92.3	44.6*	2.2	71.1	74.0*
Total Women 18–64	32.1	35.2	16.8	0.3	16.0	38.9
18–44	31.1	32.0	23.0	0.4	22.0	42.8
45–54	36.7	42.5	17.5	0.6	15.3	41.3
55–64	29.8*	41.4	9.5*	..	10.9*	28.5*

* Difference between the 18–44 and 55–64 age groups is significant in the expected direction; $p < .05$.

labor force participation at all ages. Secondary work limitations affected the level of full-time employment only after age fifty-four; younger adults with secondary work limitations had the same level of full-time employment as the nondisabled. The stability of the rate of labor force participation among severely and occupationally disabled men was largely due to the level of part-time employment. Most of the severely disabled men in the labor force worked at part-time jobs. Among the occupationally disabled the proportion in part-time jobs increased with age and the proportion unemployed decreased. Men with secondary work limitations, however, made relatively little adjustment in the nature or hours of work. The proportion employed part-time did not increase with age; more older men left the labor force rather than shifting to part-time work or continuing to seek employment.

Social Participation. Participation in household tasks and social activities was also affected by both severity of disability and age (Table 11-III). The effect of aging on social participation was relatively slight, however, compared to the effect of the severity of disability, and less consistent. The proportion with low participation in household activity was significantly larger among the severely disabled than among the partially disabled (p. < .05). The differences between age groups were statistically significant for disabled women but not for disabled men. The level of household participation was about the same for younger and older men, regardless of the severity of disability.

Social activity followed a similar pattern of declining participation with age and severity of disability (Table 11-III). The severely disabled consistently did less visiting and inviting than the partially disabled, but the effects of age on social activity, when controlled for severity of disability, were significant only for disabled women.

FINDINGS: THE RELATIONSHIP OF DISABILITY TO AGE

It is evident from these data that age and disability interact to affect the level of work participation and, to a lesser extent, household and social participation. The biological and pathological effects of aging may be examined by comparing the

TABLE 11-III
HOUSEHOLD AND SOCIAL ACTIVITY PARTICIPATION

Severity of Disability	Total	Age 18–44	45–54	55–64
	Percent With Low Household Task Participation,* of Those Disabled After Age 18			
Total Disabled	34.0	30.0	32.8	37.8†
Severe	40.6	35.5	36.1	45.2†
Occupational	31.6	32.3	30.1	32.8
Secondary	29.3	25.0	32.6	30.7
Men	45.6	43.0	44.9	48.1
Severe	58.0	61.1	51.9	59.9
Occupational	43.9	46.9	41.9	43.3
Secondary	38.7	34.2	43.8	38.1
Women	23.5	20.0	21.0	28.4†
Severe	30.2	26.2	26.8	34.2†
Occupational	20.1	17.3	18.0	24.5
Secondary	17.6	16.3	17.2	19.8
	Percent Participating in Neither Home Nor Outside Social Activities, of Those Disabled After Age 18			
Total Disabled	21.0	14.5	22.0	25.1†
Severe	30.9	22.5	32.5	33.9†
Occupational	16.3	15.6	15.0	18.5
Secondary	15.1	8.8	20.4	17.1†
Men	23.1	16.1	26.1	25.6†
Severe	40.4	36.2	48.0	38.0
Occupational	17.2	17.2	16.1	18.8
Secondary	15.9	8.6	23.0	16.2
Women	19.1	13.3	18.1	24.6†
Severe	25.2	17.6	23.2	30.8†
Occupational	15.5	13.9	13.9	18.3
Secondary	14.1	9.0	16.7	18.5†

* Less than three out of four household activities.
† Difference between the 18–44 and 55–64 age groups is significant in the expected direction; $p < .05$.

severity of disability for those with the same impairment or limitation in the different age groups. Three aspects of "health" and impairment are considered here: the major disabling condition, sickness, and functional limitations. Capacity requirements are examined in terms of occupation at the onset of disability and the nature of the work. To simplify the analysis, only the data for men are presented.

Capacity Losses. As shown in Table 11-IV, the disability rate increased with age. The rate of disability for some conditions, most notably cardiovascular disorders, however, was disproportionately higher among men aged fifty-five to sixty-four. This is a function of the increasing prevalence of certain conditions in the population with age, as well as of the extent to which conditions differ in their effect on functional capacities.

In general, the nature of the chronic condition or impairment provides little information about the loss of capacity or the likelihood of disability. The study findings, that the type of major disabling condition was not strongly related to the prevalence of disability,[18] agrees with those of a number of other studies.[19]

TABLE 11-IV

MAJOR DISABLING CONDITIONS AND THE SEVERITY OF DISABILITY

Major Disabling Condition*	Total	Men 18–44	45–54	55–64
Total Men, 18–64 (000's)	48,980	30,347	10,567	8,066
	Disability Rate Per 1,000 Population			
Disability Rate—Total	172.1	100.8	232.4	361.3
Musculoskeletal (720–749)	56.5	35.4	80.2	104.6
Cardiovascular (460–468)	40.6	13.7	60.2	116.4
Respiratory (241–245, 470–529)	21.3	15.2	24.2	40.5
Digestive (540–586)	12.9	7.2	20.8	23.9
Urogenital (590–637)	3.3	1.3	4.4	9.3
Endocrine-metabolic (250–260)	4.4	1.8	7.4	10.4
Mental (300–329)	10.0	8.1	10.8	13.8
Nervous System (330–369)	9.4	6.6	11.5	16.9
Visual Impairments (370–389)	4.3	2.7	4.6	10.0
Neoplasms (199)	2.1	†	2.7	5.7
Other and Not Specified	7.7	7.9	5.5	9.8
	Percent Severely Disabled			
Total Disabled	27.3	18.9	22.7	39.9‡
Musculoskeletal	20.9	12.0	16.6	35.5‡
Cardiovascular	26.4	16.1	13.4	39.8‡
Respiratory	21.8	7.6	25.0	39.4‡
Digestive	16.5	10.1	16.8	23.3
Urogenital	35.6	13.2	4.3	65.3‡
Endocrine-Metabolic	21.3	1.9	17.9	36.9‡
Mental	63.0	64.9	71.1	50.5
Nervous System	56.8	44.3	71.1	62.5
Visual Impairments	33.8	19.3	42.9	43.2
Neoplasms	54.9	51.9	34.5	69.6
Other and Not Specified	20.4	16.2	32.8	24.1

* *Manual of International Statistical Classification of Diseases, Injuries, and Causes of Death,* 7th revision. Geneva, World Health Organization, 1957, Vol. 1.

† Less than 1.0 per 1,000.

‡ Difference between the 18–44 and 55–64 age groups is significant in the expected direction; p < .05.

18. Haber, Lawrence D.: Epidemiological factors in disability: I. Major disabling conditions. *Social Security Survey of the Disabled,* Report Number 6. Washington, D.C., Social Security Administration, February 1969.

19. Townsend, Peter: *The Last Refuge.* London, Routledge and Kegan Paul, 1962, pp. 465–466. Morgan, James N., David, M.H., Cohen, W.J., and Brazer, H.E.: *Income and Welfare in the United States.*

Although there were variations in the severity of the disability associated with specific conditions, identification of the disabling condition did not provide a strong indication of the severity of the disability. Only a few of the major disabling conditions substantially differentiated the severity of disability; these conditions, primarily mental, nervous system and neoplastic disorders, were not, however, disproportionately represented among older disabled men. The condition classification provided, at best, a weak indication of the extent of limitation and did not explain the relationship of aging to disability. Disabled men aged fifty-five to sixty-four were consistently more likely to be severely disabled than the younger disabled men, virtually without regard to major disabling condition.

The existence of a chronic condition or impairment is not in itself a measure of the level of health or "sickness" in the population studied. Conditions may be stable or acute, active or dormant, and may or may not involve disease process. Hospitalization may be taken as a measure of sickness, as an indication that an acute, active or treatable state of illness existed during the year. Not being hospitalized does not, of course, signify a state of good health, but suggests that this group, as a whole, was not as actively ill as the hospitalized men.

TABLE 11-V
HOSPITALIZATION AND SEVERITY OF DISABILITY

Hospitalization in 1965	Total	Men 18–44	45–54	55–64
Number (000's)	8,430	3,060	2,456	2,914
Total Percent	100.0	100.0	100.0	100.0
Not Hospitalized	78.4	82.1	74.6	77.8
Hospitalized	21.5	17.9	25.4	22.1
	Percent Severely Disabled			
Total Disabled	27.3	18.9	22.7	39.9*
Not Hospitalized	24.5	17.2	20.8	35.7*
Hospitalized	37.2	26.3	28.5	55.1*

* Difference between the 18–44 and 55–64 age groups is significant in the expected direction; p <.05.

New York, McGraw-Hill, 1962, pp. 231–232. Barry, John R., and Malinovsky, M.R.: Client motivation for rehabilitation: A review. *Rehabilitation Research Monograph Series,* Number 1. University of Florida, Regional Rehabilitation Research Institute, 1965, p. 42.

Hospitalization increased only slightly with age, indicating that disabled older men were not to any great extent more actively sick than the younger men. The proportion severely disabled was significantly higher among the hospitalized than the nonhospitalized men, supporting the expectation that active illness affects the severity of disability. The relationship between age and the severity of disability was, however, relatively the same for the hospitalized and the nonhospitalized; in both groups, the proportion of older men severely disabled was about double that of men aged eighteen to forty-four. Although the active state of sickness differentiates severe disability, it did not account for the relationship of aging to the severity of disability.

The functional limitations index provides a more direct measure of the loss or reduction of capacities. The physical and self-care capacities included are common to most areas of social and work activity. Limitation in the ability to perform any of these activities would generally constitute some barrier or handicap to effective role performance. The extent to which the limitation would be considered a disability, either by the affected individual or the reciprocal role members, depends, however, on the requirements of the role or tasks, the elasticity of the environment in accepting departures from the requirements and the capacity of the individual to compensate for or adjust to losses in functional capacity. Despite the variety of activities included in the functional limitations index, the measure is, of course, not inclusive. Impairments causing fatigue, weakness, pain and memory, cognitive or sensory losses, for example, may create limitations not reflected in the physical activities. As shown in Table 11-VI, close to one-third of the disabled had no restrictions in the activities measured as functional limitations.

The severity of disability was directly related to the extent of functional limitations; the proportion severely disabled increased consistently as the extent of limitation increased. The same tendency held true for each age group, but the older men always had a higher proportion severely disabled, regardless of the extent of functional limitation. Although older men have

TABLE 11-VI
AGE AND CAPACITY DEVALUATION
FUNCTIONAL LIMITATIONS AND THE SEVERITY OF DISABILITY

Functional Limitations Index	Total	Men 18–44	Men 45–54	Men 55–54
Number (000's)	8,430	3,060	2,456	2,914
Total Percent	100.0	100.0	100.0	100.0
I. No Restriction	30.0	40.0	27.0	21.9
II. Minor	26.7	23.8	29.5	27.4
III. Moderate	21.6	16.4	27.6	21.9
IV. Severe	8.2	4.8	5.3	14.3
V. Functionally Dependent	13.5	15.1	10.6	14.4
Percent Severely Disabled				
Total Disabled	27.3	18.9	22.7	39.9*
I. No Restriction	12.9	10.4	10.7	19.9*
II. Minor	20.6	11.0	16.0	33.5*
III. Moderate	25.4	21.5	16.1	38.4*
IV. Severe	47.4	32.4	51.9	51.6
V. Functionally Dependent	63.0	47.0	74.6	73.3*

* Difference between the 18–44 and 55–64 age groups is significant in the expected direction; p <.05.

greater limitations in their functional abilities, functional limitations alone did not explain or account for the difference between younger and older disabled men in the severity of disability.

Performance Requirements—Work at Onset of Disability. The work people do represents both a set of requirements for performance and a position in the social structure. Generally, higher status positions have more flexibility in work scheduling, greater ability to manipulate requirements, and more sedentary requirements. Workers in professional, managerial and other white-collar jobs have more education and are presumed to enjoy greater security because of the relationship to organizational management and the scarcity of skills.

Unskilled and semiskilled workers, on the other hand, have heavier physical demands and less control over work requirements and scheduling. The security of their employment is often more tenuous; work becomes harder to find with increasing age and periods of unemployment last longer.

On the basis of these considerations, white-collar and skilled workers should have the lowest disability rates and unskilled and semiskilled workers should have the highest disability

rates. When occupation at onset of disability was compared
to the occupational distribution of the population of currently
employed men (Table 11-VII), fewer of the disabled had been
employed as professionals, managers, clerical and sales workers and a higher proportion had been working as craftsmen,
laborers and farmers. With the exception of craftsmen, this is
consistent with our understanding of the job requirements and
adjustment capabilities of high and low status occupations.
White-collar workers are obviously less susceptible to disability
than other workers.

The physical requirements of the job have a direct effect on
the severity of disability (Table 11-VIII). Workers engaged in
regular heavy labor at the onset of disability were significantly more likely than those with no heavy labor to become
severely disabled. The frequency of severe disability was significantly higher among the older workers in all work categories.

TABLE 11-VII

OCCUPATION AT ONSET OF DISABILITY AND SEVERITY OF
DISABILITY

Employment and Occupation	Total Employed Men, U.S., 1966*	Men Employed at Onset of Disability			
		Total	18–44	45–54	55–64
Number (000's)	42,814	6,749	1,906	2,187	2,657
Total Percent	100.0	100.0	100.0	100.0	100.0
Professional and Managers	26.6	13.9	11.2	13.4	16.3
Clerical and Sales	12.9	8.7	8.1	11.2	7.1
Craftsmen, foremen	20.0	25.2	27.1	28.4	21.2
Operatives	21.8	21.9	25.6	20.6	20.3
Service	6.5	5.8	5.7	4.7	6.6
Laborers	6.7	9.4	9.4	8.5	10.2
Farm Managers and Laborers	5.5	12.5	9.4	11.3	15.7
Occupation Unknown	...	2.6	3.3	1.8	2.7
		Percent Severely Disabled			
Total	...	26.8	16.1	20.2	39.9†
Professional and Managers	...	21.4	7.5	14.6	32.9†
Clerical and Sales	...	19.0	11.6	13.1	33.3†
Craftsmen, foremen	...	21.3	7.6	17.8	37.7†
Operatives	...	33.1	21.1	25.5	50.2†
Service	...	37.1	31.8	68.3	40.8
Laborers	...	38.4	32.8	77.4	53.3†
Farm Managers and Laborers	...	21.1	10.1	16.7	28.5†

* United States Bureau of Labor Statistics, unpublished data from the Current
Population Survey.
† Difference between the 18–44 and 55–64 age groups is significant in the expected
directions; p < .05.

TABLE 11-VIII
NATURE OF WORK AND SEVERITY OF DISABILITY

Nature of Work	Total	Men Employed at Onset of Disability		
		18–44	*45–54*	*55–64*
Number (000's)	6,749	1,906	2,187	2,657
Total Percent	100.0	100.0	100.0	100.0
Regular Heavy Labor	43.6	40.8	47.2	42.7
Occasional Heavy Labor	20.8	25.1	18.4	19.7
No Heavy Labor	30.5	28.3	30.6	32.1
Requirements Unknown	5.0	5.8	3.8	5.6
	Percent Severely Disabled			
Total Disabled	26.8	16.1	20.2	39.9*
Regular Heavy Labor	32.0	21.6	24.3	46.2*
Occasional Heavy Labor	24.6	11.9	14.6	43.8*
No Heavy Labor	20.5	11.3	16.0	29.7*

* Difference between the 18–44 and 55–64 age group is significant in the expected direction; p <.05.

The relative differences between work categories, in the proportion severely disabled, were greater, however, among young workers than among older workers, suggesting that the nature of the work becomes less important as a limiting factor with age.

The severity of disability was also related to occupational status at onset of disability, but not quite in the same way as the physical demands of the job indicate. The rate of severe disability was low among the white-collar workers and high among operatives, service workers and laborers (Table 11-VII). Both craftsmen and farm workers, however, also had low rates of severe disability, similar to those of white-collar workers. Apparently craftsmen and farmers have more control over work requirements or are in some way better able to cope with the effects of capacity limitations than other manual workers, despite the physical demands of the job.[20]

Age and severity of disability were directly related in each occupational status group. The data also indicate that interaction between occupational status and age affected the extent of the relationship to severity of disability; the differences between age groups were greater and more consistent among the high status and farm occupations than among the unskilled and semiskilled workers. This was similar to the relationship

20. Gripe, R.P. *et al.*: Returning the farmer with cardiac disease to work. *Am J Cardiol*: 354–364, March, 1961.

found between age and the nature of the work. The data may be interpreted as suggesting a reduction in job adaptability with advancing age. Higher status jobs, skilled crafts and farming have greater flexibility for adapting requirements to limitations and more transferability of skills; older workers, however, lose adaptability through diminished responsiveness, lower labor market acceptability and obsolescence of skills. Unskilled and semiskilled occupations have less flexibility, lower tolerance for physical limitation, and less capacity for transfer of skills at any age. As workers age, the differences between occupational groups in the severity of disability therefore tend to narrow.

The relationship of occupation and severity of disability might, however, also be attributed to more severe functional limitations among workers in lower socioeconomic status occupations rather than to job requirements and selection factors. The research on the relationship of social class and illness or impairment is inconclusive and shows evidence both for and against the existence of a relationship.[21]

The survey data provide some evidence of greater activity restrictions among workers in lower socioeconomic statuses (Table 11-IX). Proportionately more white-collar workers than semiskilled and unskilled workers and farmers, for example, had no restrictions in activity.

Functional limitations, however, did not account for the differences in the severity of disability associated with occupational status. Proportionately more operatives, service workers and laborers were severely disabled than workers in other occupational groups, at each level of functional limitation, although not all differences were statistically significant. The effect of occupational status on the severity of disability would therefore appear to be independent of the distribution of functional limitations among workers.

21. Antonovsky, Aaron: Social class and the major cardiovascular diseases. *J Chronic Dis, 21:* 65–106, 1968. Kadushin, Charles: Social class and the experience of ill health. *Sociological Inquiry, 34:* 67–80, Winter 1964. Mechanic, David: *Medical Sociology, A Selective View.* New York, Free Press, 1968, pp. 259–266.

TABLE 11-IX
SEVERITY OF DISABILITY BY FUNCTIONAL LIMITATIONS
AND OCCUPATIONAL STATUS

		Men Employed at Onset of Disability			
			Blue-Collar		
Functional Limitations Index	*Total*	*White-Collar*	*Craftsmen*	*Other*	*Farm*
Number (000's)	6,749	1,528	1,701	2,500	842
Total Percent	100.0	100.0	100.0	100.0	100.0
I. No Restriction	26.5	35.3	28.7	22.4	18.5
II.–III. Minor-Moderate	51.2	44.6	50.1	51.4	63.3
IV.–V. Severe-Dependent	22.0	19.4	21.1	25.8	18.3
		Percent Severely Disabled			
Total Disabled	26.8	20.5*	21.3*	35.0	21.1*
I. No Restriction	12.6	8.5*	3.9*	24.5	2.6*
II.–III. Minor-Moderate	22.6	16.4*	20.0	26.7	21.6
IV.–V. Severe-Dependent	53.7	50.8	48.2	60.4	38.3*

* Significantly different from "other blue-collar" (operatives, laborers, and service workers); $p < .05$.

Education. Although education is neither a measure of physical capacity nor of performance, it does reflect an aspect of flexibility. Education provides access to occupations and job opportunities not generally open to people with low educational attainment.[22] Years of schooling is also closely correlated with age; in the general population, men aged fifty-five to sixty-four average three years less schooling than men aged eighteen to forty-four.[23]

Disabled men show the same trend in their educational distribution; educational attainment decreases with increased age (Table 11-X). The educational level of the disabled, however, is lower than that of all men in the same age groups; low education obviously contributes to the prevalence of disability. The severity of disability is also related to educational attainment. The proportion severely disabled increases significantly as educational level drops.

At each educational level, however, the older men were more likely than the younger disabled men to be severely disabled. The differences in the proportion severely disabled were

22. Hamel, H.R.: Educational attainment of workers, March, 1966. *Monthly Labor Review:* 39–47, June, 1967.
23. U.S. Bureau of the Census: Educational attainment. *Current Population Reports,* Series 20, Number 158, 1966.

TABLE 11-X
EDUCATION AND SEVERITY OF DISABILITY

Years of Schooling Completed	Men			
		Current Age		
	Total	18–44	45–54	55–64
Number (000's)	8,430	3,060	2,455	2,914
Total Percent	100.0	100.0	100.0	100.0
Less than 9 Years	43.2	27.6	46.0	57.2
9–11 Years	18.5	18.2	22.1	15.7
12 or More Years	36.8	52.1	31.3	25.3
Not Reported	1.6	2.0	.7	1.8
	Percent Severely Disabled			
Total Men Disabled	27.3	18.9	22.7	39.9*
Less than 9 Years	40.9	37.3	33.4	47.8*
9–11 Years	20.1	19.7	13.3	28.5*
12 or More Years	15.2	8.7	12.8	31.8*

* Difference between the 18–44 and 55–64 age groups is significant in the expected direction; $p < .05$.

greater at the upper educational levels, twelve years or more of schooling, than at the lower levels. Level of education affects the severity of disability of both young and older men, but the differences between educational status groups are narrower among the older men. This is similar to the relationship of severity of disability and age with occupational status.

DISCUSSION

Examination of the data on the relationship between age and the factors affecting the severity of disability provides substantial support for the hypothesis that chronological age is a significant status characteristic for the evaluation of capability. Older disabled men consistently place a lower evaluation on their ability to work than young men with the same degree of capacity limitations, occupational background and education.

Capacity limitations and performance requirements significantly affect the prevalence of severe disability among men with limitations in the kind or amount of work they can do. The interaction between age and performance requirements also suggests that the generalized identification of chronological age as an evaluative characteristic tends to reduce adaptability and flexibility with advancing age. The differentiation of severe disability by occupational status and education was consistently smaller among older than young disabled men.

It is also possible that the higher rate of severe disability among older men is caused by a combination of factors, in which no one factor alone accounts for more than a small part of the variation. The interrelationships among age, capacity limitations and work requirements should be examined further to improve the explanation and prediction of severity of disability. The trend towards decreased differentiation between high and low status attributes with advancing age, however, suggests that the existence of complex or synergistic relationships would not invalidate the interpretation of chronological age as a unique factor for the evaluation of adaptability or acceptability.

The situations in which age is identified as a devaluating attribute are very likely to be affected by complex interrelationships of age and other variables. The employment of nondisabled men, for example, does not decrease with advancing age. Disability accounted for virtually all of reduction in the level of full-time employment after age fifty-five. Studies of employed men do not indicate a general downgrading or devaluation of older workers.[24] In the nature of orderly career patterns, experience and seniority should enhance the security and status of middle-aged and older men. As Neugarten *et al.* point out,[25] the enforcement of age norms is usually vested in the mature rather than the young. Older men generally benefit from the status and deference relationships between age groups in American society and tend to internalize the age norms to a greater degree than young men.

The age norms, however, do not provide for the disruption of or the failure to establish an orderly career pattern. Although seniority provides more job security to older workers,[26] its ad-

24. Ravin, *op. cit.;* Jaffe, *op. cit.*
25. Neugarten, Bernice L., Moore, J.W., and Lowe, J.C.: Age norms, age constraints and adult socialization. In Neugarten, Bernice L. (Ed.): *Middle Age and Aging.* Chicago, University of Chicago Press, 1968, pp. 27–28.
26. Bell, Daniel: The 'invisible' unemployed. In Nosow, S., and Form, W.H. (Eds.): *Man, Work and Society.* New York, Basic Books, 1962, pp. 149–156.

vantages are not unmixed. Seniority is also a deterrent to mobility, particularly among the semiskilled, for whom it is limited to "tenure" in a plant,[27] or a particular shop or function within a company.

The conception of occupational security in a career, through an appropriate rate of progression within an occupation, is available only to white collar and skilled workers. Semiskilled and unskilled workers tend to remain on the level at which they enter an occupation.[28]

Events which upset the age grading of managerial and professional careers, such as plant dislocation or economic contractions, also endanger job security and employability;[29] entry and intermediate level positions are usually reserved for the young and as testing grounds for mobility.

The general expectations for aging do not provide status alternatives for superannuation before retirement age. The primary alternatives for the prematurely superannuated are marginal work, as casual day labor,[30] or as "vestigial" workers floundering among a succession of short-term jobs.[31] Sheldon and Moore have commented on the instability endemic in the American job market:[32] "workers live between the threat of declining incomes and the unsettling hope of greater ones." In 1967, for example, 21 million people were hired but only 1.1 million more people were employed. Older workers represented 40 percent of the labor force and 17 percent of the un-

27. Caplow, Theodore: The Sociology of Work. Minneapolis, University of Minnesota Press, 1954, p. 108.
28. Form, William H., and Miller, D.C.: Occupational career pattern as a sociological instrument. In Nosow, S. and Form, W.H. (Eds.): Man, Work and Society. New York, Basic Books, 1962, pp. 287–295.
29. Gross, Edward: Work and Society. New York, Crowell, 1958, p. 200.
30. Caplow, op. cit., p. 93.
31. Rusalem, Herbert: The floundering period in the late careers of older disabled workers. Rehabil Lit 24: 34–40, Feb., 1963.
32. Sheldon, Eleanor B., and Moore, Wilbert E.: Indicators of Social Change: Concepts and Measurements. New York, Russell Sage Foundation, 1968, p. 124.

employed; only 5 percent of new hires, however, were forty-five or older.[33]

Age norms characterize certain forms of behavior as appropriate to specific points in the life span. Neugarten *et al.*[34] found high consensus on the behavioral characterizations of chronological ages: eighteen to twenty is the right age for young men; at forty to fifty a man is considered middle-aged; at sixty-five to seventy-five, he is old. Age thirty-five to forty is the "prime of life" for men and "most people should be ready to retire" at sixty to sixty-five. In the consensus ratings shown, age fifty to sixty was not selected as characteristic of or most appropriate for any particular activity or lifecycle stage. We may speculate from this hiatus that the fifties represent an age of ambiguity, the obverse of the adolescent dilemma of "too young to shave and too old to cry." The fifties are the boundary between the peak of involvement ("Most men hold their top jobs" at age 45–50)[35] and retirement. People who maintain their place and the outward appearance of capacity are identified as "middle-aged"; their social engagement is enhanced by the age norms and their institutional entrenchment. People who lose their place in the age-grading structure or who are labeled as impaired by disease or injury appear to be symbolically devalued, as old men, perhaps "old before their time."

The effects of impairment may be perceived as more severe when the individual is outside of an organizational setting which can redefine or adjust the capacity requirements on the basis of an existing reciprocal relationship. The physical standards for employment, for example, are more rigorous than the requirements for workers already on the job. Capacity losses may be more threatening to the older than to the younger worker, even under similar working conditions; implied differences in adaptability, return from investment in retraining and wage rate differentials limit job mobility and adjustment for older workers.

---

33. U.S. Department of Labor, *op. cit.,* pp. 21–22.
34. Neugarten, *op. cit.,* pp. 23–25.
35. *Ibid,* p. 24.

In the context of this study, the immediate consequences of age-related capability devaluation are such that a substantial proportion of older men become severely disabled who might otherwise make a more productive adjustment to disability. Employment and rehabilitation practices, however, systematically limit the adjustment opportunities of older men and negative self-evaluations lead to inflexible and maladaptive responses. Practitioners have noted the significant role that health and work attitudes play in the success or failure of work attempts among older men, regardless of the capacity loss involved or extent of physical recovery.[36]

Some studies, in Britain, have found that the emotional problems of older working men were more important factors in hard core sickness absence than the original physical condition; "it appears that if a man has three months off work at any one time in later middle-age, there is a risk he will never return to work again."[37]

For the older worker who feels his capacities devalued and his opportunities limited, the exemptions of illness and incapacity may represent the only viable alternatives to the floundering career of the vestigial worker, the downgrading of skills and the recurrent and often unavailing search for work. Role exemptions are more readily extended to older people with chronic conditions than to young adults or to those with acute illness.[38] The social rubric of disability condones withdrawal as a normatively acceptable adjustment to the situation; disability permits behavioral modifications which neither the age norms nor institutionalized hiring and retirement practices provide for before retirement age.

---

36. Forsyth, Gordon: *Doctors and State Medicine, A Study of the British Health Service.* Philadelphia, Lippincott, 1966, pp. 71–72. Gelfand, David *et al.*: Factors relating to unsuccessful vocational adjustment of cardiac patients. *J Occup Med* 2: 62–70, Feb. 1960. Welford: *Gerontologist*, 6: March 1966, *loc. cit.*

37. Forsyth, *ibid.*

38. Petroni, F.A.: The influence of age, sex and chronicity in perceived legitimacy to the sick role. *Sociology and Social Research*, 53: 180–193, Jan. 1969.

Although acceptance of disability acknowledges the devaluation of capacity, it offers more scope for normalization than the anomalous and potentially anomic condition of the older worker whose displacement from the economic system is attributed to personal failure or the operation of "cosmic" forces. As Becker comments, "the individual turns himself into the kind of person the situation demands."[39] The acceptance of disability and the requirement of proofs by regulatory agents are also consistent with increased commitment to behavior and attitudes appropriate to incapacity.

As a practical problem, there is abundant evidence that the orientation towards chronic conditions, impairments and capacity losses leads to substantial economic disenfranchisement of the displaced or disabled older worker. The common fallacy or misconception of the impairment as the disability places a distorted emphasis on the impairment as "in fact the sole or real criterion of disability...."[40] The focus on medical impairment directs attention away from performance requirements and the flexibility of requirements to the more definable but less adaptable condition or impairment.

The evidence on older worker attitudes suggests that self-regarding attitudes are fixed early in the course of incapacity; to the extent that intervention can affect the self-devaluation of older people, it should be most meaningful at the onset of incapacity, as prevention of disability, rather than as restorative treatment after the acceptance of disability. Since most of the conditions prevalent among people in late middle-age are degenerative in nature, the prospects for restoration are generally limited. As a market place of manpower orientation, the problem may be defined in terms of the utilization of capacities, rather than of service or treatment facilities. Examina-

39. Becker, Howard S.: Personal change in adult life. In Neugarten, Bernice L. (Ed.): *Middle Age and Aging.* Chicago, University of Chicago Press, 1968, p. 150.
40. American Medical Association, Committee on Medical Rating of Physical Impairment: Guides to the evaluation of permanent impairment. *JAMA. 166:* 1–109, Feb. 15, 1958, and *262:* 624–636, Nov. 13, 1967.

tion of the environment and of performance requirements offers the possibility of systematic efforts to use existing capacities more fully by adapting requirements to fit people rather than adapting people to requirements.

Methods for keeping older people in their accustomed job, through job adaptation and modification, have obvious advantages over relocation or restoration. Unfortunately, we know little about the nature of work requirements, the relationship to capacities and capacity impairment and the possibilities for adaptation of work requirements.[41] Work adaptation, however, is widely practiced by industry as a means of coping with functional impairment.[42] The data from this study also indicate the frequency of occupational adaptations to capacity limitations.

Job adaptation offers one means of "renegotiating" the evaluation of capacities for older and disabled workers. Situational adaptations which effectively or competitively use impaired capacities enhance the bargaining power of the impaired person and may affect the extent to which capacity is devalued on the basis of generalized status attributes such as chronological age.

---

41. Welford, *ibid.*, pp. 8–9.
42. See, for example, Franco, S.C.: Disability evaluation: A function of the industrial medical department. *J Occup Med 2:* 433–442, Sept. 1963.

Chapter 12

WORKMEN'S COMPENSATION AND THE OLDER WORKER

MONROE BERKOWITZ

INTRODUCTION

The excuses for not employing an applicant for a job are legion. But, whatever the reason, it is always easier to blame someone else and to claim that insurance arrangements do not allow it. Just as parents of teenagers can point to insurance rates as a justification for refusing to extend the benefits of automobile ownership to their offspring, so can the personnel manager sympathize with the plight of the older applicant by telling him that the workmen's compensation insurance company won't tolerate his being hired.

This excuse has a surface plausibility. Most of us have had some experience with insurance and the perils of cancellation. More than once we may refuse to report a minor accident lest our record with the carrier be affected. The older person also knows that he faces an increasing rate for term life insurance as he grows older. He may be well-acquainted with the difficulties those over sixty-five have had in recent years in purchasing health insurance at any price.[1]

To what extent is this a misapprehension? What are the effects of workmen's compensation programs on the hiring of the older worker? These effects depend not only on the facts, but on how these facts are interpreted by the employer and

---

1. Adverse selection, moral hazard, the structure of the market, and uncertainties may prevent transactions at any price. Kerlof, George A: The market for 'lemons': Quality uncertainty in the market mechanism. *J Economics, 84:* 488–500, Aug., 1970.

his hiring agents, be they the personnel department or the state employment service.

Misconceptions in this area die hard, but perhaps some explanation of workmen's compensation and its insurance arrangements can help dispel them. The beginning of wisdom here is to recognize that the older worker *may* be physically impaired and *may* run the risk of facing hiring obstacles on that account. The refusal to hire any person may be grounded in his lack of genuine qualifications for the job, be they skill requirements, physical stamina, or formal education. But this is an old story to anyone familiar with industrial gerontology. The problem always is to disentangle the effect that age alone has on decisions that are made at the hiring gate.

THE PLAN OF THIS ARTICLE

First we take a brief look at the origins, purposes, and general functions of workmen's compensation, with some attention to trends which contain disturbing implications for the older worker. Next we examine the sparse evidence on age and the chances of accidents. This is followed by an explanation of rate setting. A special look is taken at subsequent injury funds which relieve employers of some liability in the event of an injury to a worker with a previous disability. We examine the effect of this legislation, designed mainly to encourage the hiring of handicapped workers, but applicable to the older worker as well.

Finally we thread our way to some conclusions. Only the naive or the dishonest can claim a single truth in this complex area. We strive to strike down some misconceptions, although we are not always sure of what the exact situation is, at any given moment of time, in a given state. We begin with the ending, however, and set forth some conclusions below. The supporting detail and background follow.

CONCLUSIONS

The hiring of an older worker will never have an immediate adverse effect on an employer's insurance rates, nor will it result in the cancellation of his workmen's compensation insurance policy. Rates simply are not structured, nor are policies sold or cancelled, in this manner.

It remains true, however, that over some period of time, longer than a single policy year, any employer's insurance rate must be affected by the average experience of all employers in his so-called "class" in his state. If he is large enough, his individual plant's experience will be compared with that of the average plant in his class to determine his insurance rates.

No employer would (or should) knowingly hire an employee if the probability of that employee's falling victim to an industrial accident is extremely great. This is true regardless of the age of the employee. The question then is the extent to which accident rates or liability settlements are higher for the older worker. Our answer leads us to familiar territory. Age is not the important factor; it is physical condition, response rate to stimuli, and other physical characteristics. It is also job placement, job design, and other environmental factors. These are the things which determine the probability of an accidental injury occurring.

The evidence as to the age patterning of accidents is extremely sparse. What there is points to no greater frequency of accidents among older than among younger workers. However, there is some indication of increased severity if an accident does occur. Also, in some states, the scope of the compensation law has been broadened to include ailments which are difficult to pin down to the work place. Various degenerative diseases fall into these categories and it may be that some broadened fund ought to be introduced to take account of this trend and of possible increases in severity.

No insurance carrier will raise an employer's workmen's compensation rates because he hires older workers. The employer's rates may change over some long pull depending only on his accident frequency and severity rates and the amounts of compensation to be paid as determined by the state. If there are relationships between accident rates and the age of workers, these are not so clear and so direct as to prompt insurance carriers to take the age of workers into account in rate setting or policy cancellations.

ORIGIN AND PURPOSES OF WORKMEN'S COMPENSATION

Workmen's compensation programs were well underway in the United States by 1911, although it was not until 1948 that every state had a work injury compensation program. In this age of social security and federal involvement in manpower and social insurance programs, workmen's compensation remains exclusively a state program. Federal involvement is limited to employees of the United States Government and to the administration of the Longshoremen's and Harbor Workers' Act.

Each state law is different and generalizations must be read with this in mind. Exceptions can be found in one state or the other to any general statement about workmen's compensation. With that caution, however, we can note that under the workmen's compensation law, the worker who is injured on the job is entitled to certain medical benefits and monetary compensation, irrespective of who or what is responsible for the accidental injury. In return for making payments in all cases, regardless of whose fault it is, the employer is saved from the possibility of a law suit for injuries sustained by the worker. The worker's remedy, therefore, is an exclusive one. To be sure, the amount he will receive is limited to some portion of his actual or potential wage loss, and, in addition, his medical expenses. He will not be entitled to anything for pain or suffering, or any other psychic costs associated with his injury. Presumably, however, he will receive his stipend with a greater degree of certainty than would be the case if he took his chances in the courts.

Each employer covered under the law is obligated to make provision for the payment of these medical expenses and compensation should the need arise. These arrangements vary. Six states have exclusive state funds in which employers are obligated to insure. Twelve states have so-called competitive funds and the employer can choose to place his insurance with the state agency or make alternative arrangements. These arrangements most often consist of purchase of an insurance policy from a stock or mutual company. In all except five states and in Puerto Rico, financially responsible employers have the option of self-insurance.

As a general rule, the employer is compelled by law to insure his liability or to make some other arrangement satisfactory to the state. If his policy is cancelled by one company he must find another. In most instances state funds are obliged to accept everyone. States without exclusive or competitive funds have some sort of assigned risk plan, or some other arrangement for employers who have difficulties in buying a policy.

TRENDS IN WORKMEN'S COMPENSATION

This is not the place to dwell on what is wrong with our system of workmen's compensation. Among its major deficiencies are the following:[2]

1. Limited medical benefits in some states.
2. The low level of weekly cash benefit allowances.
3. Many workers are not covered in some states.
4. Many occupational diseases are not covered.
5. Rehabilitation of workers is not a prime objective.
6. Minor permanent disabilities take too large a portion of the benefit dollar.
7. The system has become too legalistic and litigious.

In addition to these fairly obvious deficiencies, there is another problem which does not lend itself to any easy solution. It simply was a good bit easier in 1911 (or at least everyone thought it was) to distinguish between accidental injuries which were the result of an on-the-job incident or condition, and those which were the result of an occurrence or condition off the job. The archetypal case of workmen's compensation is

---

2. The academic critics are many but their collective voice may be less impressive than a single voice from the insurance industry. The seven points cited are abstracted from "Workmen's Compensation in Crisis," a statement of position by Clarence G. Johnson, Senior Vice President and Secretary of the Industrial Indemnity Corporation (published by the company, San Francisco, 1970). I agree with Mr. Johnson's indictment but not with his prescription for a cure.

the traumatic injury which results in some obvious orthopedic disability. But, as the scope of the laws was broadened in some states to include occupational diseases and other less specific ailments, the distinction between ailments whose origin was in the industrial environment from others has become almost impossible.

Radiation injuries, heart and circulatory system failures, back injuries, psychiatric complaints, and lung diseases all figure prominently in workmen's compensation cases. Each can have an industrial origin, but each can arise in other ways as well.

The older worker may be especially affected by some of these impairments. The employer located in a jurisdiction which has exhibited leniency and generosity toward workers by granting awards in marginal cases where industrial origin is in doubt may face the problem by raising arbitrary age barriers at the hiring gate. This difficult problem may affect all age groups, but be particularly hard on an older worker. Some sort of subsequent injury fund may be appropriate here, but before considering this we examine the general evidence on age and accidents.

ACCIDENT RATES AND AGE

The crucial question is whether older people do in fact have more compensable accidents than younger workers. Simple questions such as these have a way of ending up with complex answers. As in any other type of work injury question, both frequency and severity rates are involved. The frequency rate is the number of work injuries per million man hours worked. An injury can be either disabling or nondisabling, and most of the data on frequency rates are cast in terms of disabling injuries. A disabling injury is one in which the employee either sustains some permanent impairment or is disabled for at least one full shift beyond the day of injury. Nondisabling injuries require only first-aid treatment. The severity of the injuries is measured by the number of days for which workers are forced to absent themselves from work because of the disability. This is supplemented by a series of arbitrary time charges to take account of deaths and permanent impairments.

Apparently the older workers tend to have lower frequency rates than do younger workers, although if an older worker is involved in an injury, the severity tends to be greater. Comprehensive studies are rare in this area. An analysis of the work records of nearly eighteen thousand workers in a variety of manufacturing industries showed an injury frequency rate of 9.7.[3]

For workers between twenty and twenty-four the rate was only 4.0 injuries per million man hours worked. This climbed steadily and those between ages forty and forty-four had an injury frequency rate of 12.4. This tended to decline until workers sixty to sixty-four had an injury frequency rate of 9.5 and those between fifty-five to fifty-nine a rate of 10.1, close to the average for the group.

If we look, however, at the average days of disability we find that these range as high as 23.4 for those between twenty and twenty-four. This rate tends to fall in the middle age groups of thirty-five to thirty-nine, and then does tend to climb. As the worker grows older the average days of disability do tend to increase.

Nondisabling injuries show almost the same story. The frequency rate falls off with age and the average number of visits to the physician for the nondisabling injury shows a slight tendency to increase with age.

There is some other evidence which indicates a difference in the type of accidents encountered by people of varying ages. A British sample of two thousand agricultural accidents showed very little age patterning for the overall rate. However, accidents preventable by judgment tended to decrease by age, whereas accidents preventable by rapid response to sudden events tended to increase.[4]

The National Safety Council's data on deaths due to ma-

---

3. Kossoris, Max D.: Absenteeism and injury experience of older workers. *Monthly Labor Review, 90:* 16–19, July, 1967.
4. King, H.F.: An age-analysis of some agricultural accidents. *Occup Psychol* 29:245–253, cited in Riley, Matilda White *et al.: Aging and Society.* New York, Russell Sage Foundation, 1969, vol. 2, p. 433.

chinery accidents show that the rate has a tendency to peak at ages forty-five to sixty-four, although when we look at all accidental deaths, the rate is higher in ages fifteen to twenty-four than in ages forty-five to sixty-four.[5]

It is difficult to balance out frequency and severity; they are different things and the insurance rate-making procedures take this difference into account. Older workers on the average have fewer accidents per million man hours of work than do younger workers. If this is too strong a statement, then it can be said that there is no good evidence which correlates age with the frequency of accidents.

We cannot be satisfied with these data on age patterning of accidents. Older workers may have lower accident rates than younger workers because of the selection of older workers who are kept on the job. This may be of no great help to applicants for jobs. The differences may also arise because of different exposure rates. Only younger workers may be put on jobs where higher risks are involved.[6]

The facts of the matter may not be as important as what people believe the facts to be. Personnel workers at a midwestern producer of bearings and other metal products, employing almost 8,500 workers, claimed older workers are more prone to injuries causing hernias or back trouble, and that they are not likely to recover as readily as younger workers. As Brennan, Taft, and Schupack put it, "Whether such views can be statistically validated is not significant so long as the belief is a basis of policy."[7]

Another personnel man interviewed from a company employing 26,000 workers in the metals, ferrous mining and smelting industry did not believe that the older worker was any less productive than his younger competitor; he also believed that the older worker's lower absenteeism, regularity of attendance, and greater conservativeness and willingness to accept disci-

5. National Safety Council: *Accident Facts.* Chicago, National Safety Council, 1969, pp. 6, 7, 14, and 15.
6. Brennan, Michael, Taft, Philip, and Schupack, Mark: *The Economics of Age.* New York, W.W. Norton & Co. Inc., 1967, p. 39.
7. Brennan, Michael, Taft, Philip, and Schupack, Mark: *Ibid.,* p. 67.

pline made him a greater asset. However, he regarded fringe benefits as an impediment, "Health, pensions and welfare plans, and especially workmen's compensation costs tend to make the older worker less desirable at the unskilled job levels."[8]

WORKMEN'S COMPENSATION INSURANCE PRICING[9]

Employers pay for workmen's compensation insurance according to $100 of payroll. An employer is placed in a so-called "class" according to his business operations. Each of these classes has a particular manual rate, and for approximately 85 percent of employers, this is the rate that will be paid.[10] The other 15 percent will be experience rated and receive rate reductions, or increases, depending on their experience with accidents. The importance of this minority of employers is attested to by the fact that they pay about 85 percent of all premiums collected.

Our principal question is whether the hiring of older workers will increase the insurance rates. One way to get at this is to ask the question of why an employer may be required to pay higher rates in one year than in another year. To determine whether a rate change is indicated, the experience of all employers in the state is combined, and the losses (the cost of compensation and medical benefits of all employers in some past period of time) are contrasted with the so-called permissible loss ratio. In effect this is the amount of the total premium

---

8. Brennan, Michael, Taft, Philip, and Schupack, Mark: *Ibid.*, p. 69.
9. We present a general description of workmen's compensation pricing in its most schematic form. Additional information can be obtained from various sources. An excellent source for a summary description is Williams, Jr., Arthur C.: *Insurance Arrangements Under Workmen's Compensation.* Washington, D.C., U.S. Department of Labor, Wage and Labor Standards Administration, Bureau of Labor Standards, Bulletin No. 317, 1969, pp. 67–94. Williams' explanation contains references to other more comprehensive explanations of workmen's compensation insurance rate making.
10. In addition to the so-called manual rates, small employers may be required to pay an expense or loss constant. In addition there is a minimum premium requirement corresponding to the premium that would be developed if his payroll were $2,500 per year.

that must be set aside to pay for losses, i.e. cash compensation and cost of medical services. The balance of the premium is allocated for expenses of the insurance carrier. These include taxes, acquisition expenses, costs of safety inspection, and other services provided by the carrier. It would not be too far afield to think of the total premium as being composed of about a 60 percent loss portion and a 40 percent expense premium.

If the permissible loss ratio is greater than actual losses, a rate decrease may be in order. If the experience exceeds the expected portion, then a rate increase is proposed. Once the proposed *general* rate level change is determined, the next step is examining the experience of each of the classes.

The losses of each class are divided into three categories. One is the serious losses. These include the death, permanent total and the so-called major permanent partial disabilities. Second are the nonserious losses which are all other disabilities, and third are the medical expenses. These actual losses per $100 of payroll are contrasted with the so-called formula pure premiums. In its simplest terms this is the amount needed to pay the indicated losses, once they are adjusted to eliminate chance factors.

Adjustments are now made for changes in payrolls and certain other minor factors to determine the manual rate for a particular class. In essence then, rates are based upon the loss experience of all employers in the state and the particular loss experience of other employers in the same class. This rate will change up and down on a year-to-year basis depending on these factors.[11]

The larger employers qualify for experience rating and this means that there will be a further adjustment based upon the individual employer's experience. The cut-off point varies, but it is safe to think of those employers who would pay average annual premiums at manual rates of about $750 as those who

---

11. About half of workmen's compensation premiums written are derived from policies that provide for payment of dividends. Although for the most part these dividends are returned on some uniform basis, some insurers alter rate relativities by varying dividend rates.

are experience rated. These employers are large enough to have "credible" experience in their own shops. The amounts they will pay as workmen's compensation premiums can be lower or higher than their class premiums, depending on whether their experience is better or worse than the experience of the average employer in their class.

One modification of this generality is important for our purposes. In the rather complex formula used to figure experience rates, more weight is assigned to the relative frequency of losses than to the relative dollar value which is a measure of severity. Even for those employers who are experience rated, the hiring of an older worker should not have a major impact on rates if, as has been alleged earlier, the older workers tend to have fewer accidents, although, when accidents occur, the resultant injury may be more severe. The insurance rate makers, for quite different reasons, tend to weigh frequency more heavily than severity. Their reasoning is that severity is much less predictable.[12]

Some large employers (the size differs in different states) are given permission to self-insure. These employers must be in sound financial condition and be of a minimal size, as measured either by payroll or by the number of employees. Some states require self-insurers to make deposits, others do not. Although the self-insurer may have reinsurance for some catastrophic losses, he must be concerned with the frequency and severity of all accidents that occur in his plant for which

---

12. Large employers also qualify for premium discounts, and may be retrospectively rated. Experience rating relates premiums paid to experience sometime in the past. Retrospective rating, on the other hand, relates premiums to the employer's experience during the policy period. In effect, he pays a deposit at the beginning of the year and then his actual rates are adjusted based upon his current experience. Employers must develop a standard premium of at least $1,000 to be eligible for retrospective rating. This becomes a type of quasi self-insurance with the employer paying for the losses and in addition a fee to the insurance carrier for servicing the employer. Certain maximum and minimum premiums are provided and the employer may choose one of several different plans.

claims are paid. The entire amount of any loss is paid directly by him.

This is hardly an exhaustive discussion of workmen's compensation rate making; however, enough has been said to make the point that there is no direct effect on rates when an employer hires older workers. If the hiring of older workers does have an effect on rates, it is at best an indirect one. With few exceptions, an employer's rates will not be affected immediately, or directly, since he pays his insurance premium based upon $100 of payroll, and based upon past experience of employers in the state and in his classification. Only if he is large enough to have his rate based on the experience in his own plant, or if he is a self-insurer, will the impact of a loss be felt directly.

SUBSEQUENT INJURY FUNDS

Any discussion of the hiring of the impaired worker, or the older worker, or anyone else with some marginal disadvantage, turns eventually to the notion of a fund which will relieve the employer of any excess liability. Theoretically, the existence of these funds should make the employment prospects of the older worker brighter.

The basic purpose of most existing funds is to relieve the employer of any additional liability if an employee with a pre-existing disability suffers a work injury. The classic case, and unfortunately one of the few cases where such funds have any usefulness, is the one-armed worker. If he suffers an accident in which he loses his other arm, he would end up permanently and totally disabled under the workmen's compensation laws. The question now arises, what is the employer liable for? In one sense, the accident was one in which the employee lost an arm and it could be argued that this is all the employer should be liable for. However, the employee is left permanently and totally disabled, a condition which calls for greater monetary compensation than does the loss of an arm. The solution in most states is to make the employer liable only for the loss of the one arm, but then to compensate the employee for permanent and total disability. The difference between the employer's liability and the amounts the employee receives is paid from the subsequent injury fund.

For the most part these funds are financed by some assessment on all carriers or self-insured employers. No matter how financed, this payment, in effect, becomes a liability of all employers, rather than of the individual employer.

Theoretically, this arrangement is preferable to the alternatives of having the employee waive his rights under the law, or attempting to apportion the loss in such a way that it is divided between the employer and the worker. Both such arrangements deny the purpose of workmen's compensation as a social insurance program.

There are many problems with these funds. Some of the difficulties can be listed.

1. Coverage tends to be limited as to the type of injuries covered for the pre-existing condition and also, and most important, for the eventual condition. Under the laws of some states, an employee must become permanently and totally disabled before he can collect under the fund.

2. Typically there are fairly cumbersome administrative arrangements which make it difficult for the fund to be used when needed.

3. There are limitations in some states which prevent an employee from collecting if the second injury is the result of an aggravation, activation, or "lighting up" of his pre-existing condition.

Even if subsequent injury funds worked well, they still do not meet the essential problems of the older worker. There is the possibility of devising a fund which might help. The same injury to the man in his twenties and the man in his fifties may result in a different loss of work time and medical expenses. If this is so, and if we enter into a judgment that the hiring of older workers is socially useful, then we might say that any extra costs incurred ought to be a liability of the state as a whole.

Most subsequent injury funds are fairly narrowly financed by employers but there is no real reason why there could not be contributions from general revenues. What is needed is a scheme whereby older workers would be given payments from this fund for that portion of the cost of the injury which is over and above what the costs would be for an average worker with the usual healing time.

It is also possible to think of such a fund as absorbing the major portion of the liability for those cases where the origin of the condition is obscure.

The possibility of any change in workmen's compensation laws is not great.[13] Such a change might have to come on some uniform basis among the states and this has proved to be an almost impossible task. However, there is the precedent of the so-called "black lung" legislation for miners, whereby federal arrangements are overriding state schemes for miners with particular lung conditions.[14] Federal legislation for older workers might face this problem directly by financing some experiments to see whether it is possible to devise such a scheme. It would be necessary for the fund to assume only the differential costs associated with the possibly longer healing period of the older worker. The basic costs of the injury would remain the liability of the employer.

The very existence of such a fund would serve to dispel the psychological barriers now working against the employment of the older worker.

---

13. An excellent special fund provision has been proposed by the Council of State Governments, but in spite of assiduous promotion since at least 1965, few states have responded by changing their legislation. The so-called "model law" provision would go a long way toward meeting the problem of the older worker although its effects would still be confined to a second or subsequent injury. Just a listing of the twenty-six "permanent physical impairments" indicates their applicability to the older worker. Among these are the following: diabetes, cardiac disease, arthritis, Parkinson's disease, cerebral vascular accident, psychoneurotic disability following treatment in a recognized medical or mental institution, hemophilia, chronic osteomyelitis, ankylosis of joints, hyperinsulism, muscular dystrophies, arteriosclerosis, thrombophlebitis, varicose veins and ruptured intervertebral disk. *Workmen's Compensation and Rehabilitation Law*. Chicago, Illinois, The Council of State Governments, 1965.

14. Federal Coal Mine Health and Safety Act of 1969. Title IV.

As has been stated, it is not so much what the actual facts are, but rather what personnel and employment managers believe them to be. The existence of a functioning subsequent injury fund would take the wind out of the sails of the objection that workmen's compensation costs would be increased by the hiring of the older worker. Even if the fund were never used, it might serve to dispel this one argument mitigating against the older worker's employment.

CONCLUSIONS AGAIN

The basic conclusions have been set forth in the beginning and need not all be repeated here. One can't escape the feeling that an increase in workmen's compensation rates is used as an excuse, rather than the real reason for not hiring job applicants who are in the middle and upper age ranges. Even a casual look at how workmen's compensation rates are set would prove that the hiring of older workers will have no direct effect on the rates. An employer will pay a rate based upon the experience of all employers in a state, in general, and other employers in his same insurance class, in particular. About 15 percent of the employers will feel a more direct impact, but even here the experience rating formula is one which weighs frequency heavier than severities, and it is with the former that the older worker has the better experience.

There is always the danger of being guilty of a fallacy of composition. What may not be true for the individual employer in the immediate short-run period may be true of all employers over some longer pull. If older workers in general do have more injuries, this will be reflected in insurance rates. All losses are eventually paid by employers; the insurance rates only spread them out among all employers in certain predetermined ways. It is also true that if workmen's compensation insurance laws are interpreted to encompass conditions and diseases which are found more frequently among older than younger workers, there might be a reluctance to hire older workers. This stems in part from the difficulty of trying to distinguish whether such conditions are work connected or not. The solution may be to give up trying to make the distinction, but this is a more fundamental change than can be discussed here.

It is apparent that those who are interested in promoting the employment of the older worker will have to emphasize over and over again the individuality of the older worker, and that he must be evaluated in terms of the jobs available to him. If the older worker is more dependable and reliable, but less agile and less responsive to stimuli, the answer may well lie in the encouragement of intelligent job placement.

Those firms which are conscientious about job placement ought not to be penalized, directly or indirectly, if they follow both the letter of the law and optimal social policy, by hiring older workers. If existing arrangements under subsequent injury funds are not sufficient, alternative arrangements can easily be devised so that even the possibility of an increase in workmen's compensation costs because of the age of the worker can be dissipated.

VI. GOVERNMENTAL ENCOURAGEMENT
FOR THE MIDDLE-AGED

Chapter 13

TRENDS IN LEGISLATION AFFECTING OLDER WORKERS: TAKING THE LONG VIEW

THEODOR SCHUCHAT

By the tens of thousands, bills are introduced at each session of Congress. Each year, committee hearings consider a few score, and several dozen are enacted. Why does a legislator introduce a measure that he knows will not receive a hearing by the committee designated to appraise it? Why do some bills languish in the legislative halls for decades, only to move suddenly and rapidly through the labyrinth toward enactment as if they had been given an unseen and wholly arbitrary impetus? What is the process by which the public policy formulations of scholars and practitioners in a new field of interest, such as industrial gerontology, eventually become the law of the land?

It is customary to explain the legislative process as the continuing competition of contending economic and social forces, an explanation that is widely accepted because the mass media focus attention on the gladiatorial aspects of law-making.[1] Combat is necessary to secure enactment of significant legislation, and the intricacies, not to mention the etiquette, of this competition should not be overlooked.[2] Yet however interest-

1. Scholars have also taken this view: see, for example, Bailey, Stephen K.: *Congress Makes A Law*. New York, Columbia University Press, 1950, a classic account of the Employment Act of 1946. A journalistic chronicle of the long effort to realize Medicare, which is to my mind incomplete, is Harris, Richard: *A Sacred Trust*. New York, New American Library, 1966.
2. An excellent explanation of the way Congress works is Gross, Bertram: *The Legislative Struggle*. New York, McGraw-Hill, 1953, but note also Froman, Jr., Lewis A.: *The Congressional Process: Strategies, Rules, and Procedures*. Boston, Little, Brown, 1967. Less dispassionate is Bendiner, Robert: *Obstacle Course on Capitol Hill*. New York, McGraw-Hill, 1964.

ing or memorable the enactment of a measure may be, it is simply the climax of a long spectacle, the climactic scene of the pageant, as it were, which has been preceded by several others and will be followed by one or more anticlimaxes and an epilogue. To play a part, or even to appreciate the drama fully, one must enter the theater long before the peak of emotion and conflict that is represented by the decisive roll-call vote of legislators.

Elizabeth Wickenden, who has coached many an actor on this stage and ghost-written numerous scripts, some notably successful, has analyzed the "decades of evolving thought and widening support" that come before and after the dramatic *denouement*.[3] To continue the figure, she has identified the seven acts into which every drama of social legislation is inherently divided, seven phases that are well-recognized by its authors, directors, and actors. Her analytic framework will be described and exemplified by legislative proposals and enactments in behalf of older people.

The first period identified by Miss Wickenden is that of "the generative change," a basic alteration in society that can be expected to produce further massive alteration. Our example would be the demographic shift first evident in this country four decades ago which indicated that both the number and proportion of older people were going to grow with relative rapidity. Today we are well aware that this demographic change presaged many social and economic developments, a train of consequences whose end is by no means in sight, but very few people are so discerning during the first phase of social change. During the 1930's, when nearly a third of the labor force was for a time on the public assistance rolls, the plight of the older worker first became apparent to many.

The second period is characterized by growing awareness of human need resulting from the basic social change. E. W. Burgess, for example, ignited academic interest in what later became known as social gerontology in 1943 when he was chairman of the Social Science Research Council's Committee on

---

3. Wickenden, E.: Social action. *Encyclopedia of Social Work*, 15:697–703, 1965.

Social Adjustment. This group fostered a Committee on Social Adjustment in Old Age which, in turn, issued a research planning report in 1948. "From this point forward," Clark Tibbitts has written,[4] "there has been considerable development of research and training facilities." Certain memorable episodes during this period create lasting attitudes, e.g. the closing of the Packard plant in 1956, which left many older workers without either jobs or pensions. This also is the period of the polemicist or muckraking journalist who describes social problems in terms of individual cases or with amateurish data.

This period, which Miss Wickenden terms one of "emergence of need," is succeeded by that characterized by the "proposition of solutions." The distinction is not necessarily clear-cut chronologically, and the same individual may both indicate need and suggest a solution, but such cases are rare. The first bill to outlaw age-discrimination in employment was introduced in Congress in 1957, although the campaign to enact such a measure was begun by the Fraternal Order of Eagles in 1942, and by 1955 three states had enacted statutes. By the time the Age-Discrimination in Employment Act was signed by the President at the end of 1967, twenty-three states and Puerto Rico had similar laws on their books, half of these enacted after 1960. A much longer drama began when the National Health Insurance Program was enacted in Great Britain in 1911. This evoked considerable interest in trade union and academic circles on this side of the Atlantic to which may be traced the enactment, ultimately, of the Medicare legislation.[5]

The fourth stage is that of "debating the proposals." We are now in this stage with respect to legislation imposing stronger and more detailed social controls over private pension plans. The problems have been acknowledged. The interest of refor-

4. Tibbitts, C.: Origin, scope, and field of social gerontology. *Handbook of Social Gerontology.* Chicago, University of Chicago Press, 1960, p. 6.
5. For a short history of the events leading to the enactment of Medicare, in which the stages outlined here may be plainly distinguished, see: Corning, Peter A.: *The Evolution of Medicare From Idea to Law.* Washington, U.S. Department of Health, Education, and Welfare, 1969.

mers has been gained, scholars have published a number of descriptive and analytic works, and various bills have been introduced. These legislative proposals have been the subject of several Congressional committee hearings and the report of a Cabinet Committee. Both the Johnson and Nixon administrations have submitted legislative recommendations of their own. These bills are being studied by the private interest groups that would be affected and by the public interest groups that represent the civic conscience.

Next comes the "time for decisive action." Differing viewpoints are reconciled and compromises developed. Bills begin to receive more serious consideration by Congressional Committees. Broad public support is awakened by public relations campaigns. Presidents call for enactment of proposals, or perhaps their delay or defeat, in special messages to Congress. Bills may be enacted by one branch of government but not another, as occurred last year with the program for middle-aged and older workers that was added by the Senate to the Manpower Development and Training Act Amendments that were later vetoed by the President. In this period, it is clear that legislation cannot be long delayed, and the period comes to a close with enactment of the consensual legislative proposal that was developed in the preceding period or a significant portion or variation of it.

Two more periods ensue. After the new law is on the books, the administrative agencies of government begin their "execution of policy."[6] The Age Discrimination in Employment Act is in this period. The dimensions of the remedial or alleviative program authorized by the law may be restricted by appropriation of insufficient funds, and the law's proponents must therefore persuade the legislature to support the statute. Friends of the program must be alert, also, lest it be vitiated by appointment of unsympathetic administrators. They must be willing, for instance, to bring court actions that test the limits of their new powers and resolve ambiguities in the new law.

As the new program accumulates data and experience, it be-

---

6. One of the rare descriptions of this period is Bailey, Stephen K.: *ESEA: The U.S. Office of Education Administers a Law.* Syracuse, Syracuse University Press, 1968.

comes apparent that the law needs perfecting. Perhaps the statute proves to be inadequate and other measures recommend themselves. Thus we arrive at the last period of "advance to new problems." Medicare and Medicaid illustrate this period. In the light of experience, Congress expanded Medicare benefits and turned away from state administration of Medicaid.

Since this discussion is of social phenomena, it should be remembered that the periods merge into one another; some of the actors may be reciting the lines of a previous act, so to say, after the curtain has been raised on a later one. One period may seem to be interminable, either because public concern is not yet intense or because diverse views have not yet been reconciled or perhaps merely because effective leadership has not yet appeared. Sooner or later, though, one phase gives way to the next, sometimes with astonishing speed.

Finally, it should be kept in mind that all the phases are manifest simultaneously. Once Miss Wickenden's conceptual framework has been grasped, it is not difficult to survey the contemporary scene and place various social problems in their appropriate category. The significance of a Ralph Nader is appreciated immediately from this perspective, as is the sponsorship of a novel legislative proposal, the formation of a group to press for legislation, or the appointment of a "task force" by the Executive Branch.

The utility, then, of Miss Wickenden's formulation is that, upon reflection, one may decide upon the most fruitful course of action with respect to a specific social problem. Does it require a seer or social research, a creative solution or merely a legislative draftsman, a muckraker or a mass membership organization? Can social change be effected in this session of Congress, in this Presidential term, or in this decade? To achieve social progress without wasted motion or lost time, judgments of this kind must be made.

Chapter 14

OLDER WORKERS IN CANADA: EMPLOYMENT, TRAINING, AND RETIREMENT

IAN CAMPBELL

Canada is a vast land, larger in area than the United States. It has a population of some twenty-one million people, approximately one-tenth of the population of the United States. Most of our inhabitants live in the southern part of the country with a high concentration in Ontario and Quebec around the Great Lakes complex. This fact means that the majority of Canadians live farther south than the northern border of the United States, so that the opinion so generally held in the United States that Canada is a forbidding and cold country is not entirely true. We do have a vigorous winter climate with its attendant association with winter sports, but we also have extensive vineyards and peach orchards that attest to the warmth which we experience in the summer.

Our original French and British stock has been enriched by in-comers from all over the world, bringing with them the contributions of their various cultures. The growing importance of our oil and mineral resources and expanding industry add to the wealth derived from agricultural and forestry products.

Our people are protected against want by social welfare programs, and health services include hospital coverage in all provinces and medicare programs in seven with the expectation that all will be covered in the very near future.

Administratively, we have a federal-state structure, divided into ten provinces and the Yukon and Northwest Territories. Jurisdictionally, each province is responsible for the health, welfare and education of its own people. Federal contributions encourage equality of service. Unlike the United States, the operation of the employment service is a federal responsibility. The rationale here is that the economy of the country can best be developed in an atmosphere that does not overemphasize provincial boundaries.

The Department of Manpower and Immigration, through its five Regional Directors General, operates some 350 Canada Manpower Centres across Canada dedicated to matching jobs and workers and to improving the quality and skills of our labor force and the best utilization of manpower resources.

In keeping with this mandate, there is in Departmental headquarters, in the Manpower Utilization Branch, a Section on Older Workers. The staff of this section gathers and disseminates information on the employment, training and retirement of older workers, from national and international sources. In this way, a continuing educational program presenting factual information concerning the employment potential of middle-aged and older workers is carried out. With permission from authors and publishers, important publications or articles are reviewed, summarized and distributed to appropriate audiences. As an example, a condensation of OECD material which we titled "Ergonomics—What Is It? What Can It Do?" was distributed widely to employers.

The section staff assures that the Canada Manpower Centres (CMC's), through the Regions, constantly endeavor to apprise employers of the valuable contribution to be made to the economy by the older work force. Discriminatory practices are discouraged by advocating that hiring be done on the basis of qualifications regardless of chronological age.

At various times, we have used national billboard campaigns, radio, television and the printed word, as well as ministerial letters to employers asking for cooperation in utilizing older manpower. Two of our provinces, British Columbia and Ontario, have Age Discrimination legislation. In Ontario, an Act prohibits employment discrimination because of age against persons forty to sixty-five years old. British Columbia's Human Rights legislation has been extended beyond the normal provisions which prohibit discrimination because of race, color or creed to include discrimination because of age.

While encouraging the concept that workers should be hired on the basis of their worth, we have tended to focus our efforts, as far as employment is concerned, on the forty-five to sixty-five age group. It is in this period that a worker should be at the peak of his earnings, able to meet his family responsibilities for housing, care, and education, and to lay the foundation for adequate living in his later years. Indeed, his ability to provide for other than a marginal existence after retirement depends largely on his degree of successful participation in the labor force in his forties and fifties.

What then is the employment situation of middle-aged and older workers in Canada? In January, 1970, with a labor force of just over 8 million, 2.6 million or almost one-third were over forty-five years of age. Fortunately, most of this group are steadily employed, often at the peak of their earnings and productivity. The unemployment rate for workers in the forty to sixty-five age bracket is lower than the average rate for all ages. To be specific, the 1969 average rate of unemployment for all ages was 4.7 percent; while the average rate was higher in the fourteen to nineteen and twenty to twenty-four age groups, it reached a low of 3.3 percent for the thirty-five to fifty-four group, increased to 4.1 percent for fifty-five to sixty-four, and equalled the national average of 4.7 percent for persons sixty-five and over. The rates in the older group are, therefore, comparatively low, but there is an increase in incidence of unemployment in the fifty-five to sixty-four age group.

Once unemployed, middle-aged and older workers tend to remain unemployed for longer periods than the younger age groups. Frequently, older persons must return to employment at a lower level than they had previously enjoyed with disastrous effects on their morale and financial situation. Layoffs may be associated with declining physical capacity, or with the obsolescence of skills. This fact has influenced our training policies.

Prior to 1967, the Government of Canada, in the economic interest of the country, encouraged the expansion of vocational training facilities and opportunities by assuming a large percentage of the costs incurred by the provinces in this field.

After passage of the Adult Occupational Training Act in 1967, a different posture was assumed. The federal government withdrew from the sharing of vocational training costs within the regular school system and assumed the total cost of occupational training for adults through the Canada Manpower Training Program. To avoid encouraging withdrawal from the school system, the government assumes the cost of training only if the individual is beyond school leaving age and has been out of the school system for one year. Allowances, or "income replacement" as we prefer to call them, can only apply when the individual has had three years attachment to the labor force or has one or more dependents. Attachment to the labor force includes situations such as undergoing treatment, receiving rehabilitation service, or being incarcerated, i.e. conditions which would make normal employment impossible. Referrals to training are made by the Canada Manpower Centres and the criteria are that the provision of further training has a vocational objective and is likely to improve the individual's competitive position in the labor market, or to increase his earning capacity.

How does the program work? The Government of Canada purchases training places from the provinces in relation to the demands of the labor market. The full cost of services, including amortization of building costs, teaching staff, and materials, is assumed by the federal government. Individuals are then assigned to appropriate places and during the period of training receive an allowance which can vary from $40.00 a week to $103.00 depending upon the number of dependents. In addition to regular skill training, where required the individual can receive sufficient upgrading in communication skills, mathematics, and science to qualify him for entry to further skill training. Academic upgrading can extend over a fifty-two-week period and skill training is limited to a similar period. It is hoped that by making use of these provisions many more workers will take advantage of the opportunity to return to training and keep their skills current. The problems now encountered by many older workers through obsolescence of skills will be lessened.

While there are still many minor problems to be solved in

this program, the general effect has been good. The number of people receiving training has increased greatly and the average age of those participating shows a tendency to become higher each year. Last year, over 300,000 persons took advantage of this training and the majority was involved in full-time training. While the participation from the older age groups is not yet as high as we would like, in the fiscal year 1968 to 1969 more than twelve thousand of those who received training were over forty-five years of age. While there is no barrier because of age, the assumption still persists that formal training is for the young only. Middle-aged workers themselves are sometimes reluctant to undergo classroom training and need counseling to raise their self-confidence and convince them that they too can learn.

And so in Canada, the normal employment services of counseling, referral, and placement are supplemented by an extensive retraining program that constantly seeks to keep abreast of technological change by providing workers with an opportunity to upgrade their skills. Where retraining or job opportunities do not exist in a particular area, workers and their families can be moved to other localities where such opportunities are available. In other cases, it is possible to call upon community resources or the federal-provincial Vocational Rehabilitation Program for pre-employment services.

Recently, there has been an increase in unemployment rates which has increased the trend, common in North America, toward retirement at sixty-five and even earlier.

We must, therefore, look with added concern at the 1,750,-000 Canadians aged sixty-five and over. Retirement in most cases is no longer a question of personal choice. It is no longer a luxury chosen by those who can afford it. Compulsory retirement has become standard practice in business and industry. Continual employment until retirement age is reached has become even more important.

I cannot, in this short paper, deal with the many new situations that this phenomenon creates. How do we help the retired person to meet the psychological and marital stresses that this implies and how do we deal with the vexing question of how to employ leisure time in a meaningful way? While provision for the economic needs of the older sector does not in itself solve the problems, the decline in the incidence of opportunity to work vests the economic aspects with primary importance.

Fortunately, the formerly much-used excuse that pension plans prevented the hiring of older workers in the preretirement group is no longer completely valid. Two plans now intermesh to provide all Canadian citizens with a measure of financial security after they reach sixty-five years of age.

The Old Age Security program has been in existence since 1952. Originally payable to all Canadians on reaching seventy years of age, the qualifying age has been reduced over the past five years and is now payable regardless of income, starting at age sixty-five. The monthly payment has gradually increased from $40.00 to $79.58 now, with a recently enacted escalator clause tying payments to the consumer price index. A guaranteed income supplement in cases of need may provide an additional amount to assure a minimum income of $111.41 per month.

In many cases the Old Age Security program is supplemented by private pension plans. In addition, the Canada Pension Plan which became effective on January 1, 1966, and its counterpart in the Province of Quebec, the Quebec Pension Plan, together provide virtually universal coverage to all workers in Canada aged eighteen years to age seventy who have employee status or are self-employed. Both plans are interlocking, with portability, vesting and locked-in pension credits.

The Canada and Quebec Pension Plans pay benefits to participants at age sixty-five only if the participants discontinue regular employment. Since these plans have been in existence for only five years, there is an inducement for participants to continue working beyond age sixty-five in order to build up additional pension credits. This inducement will, of course, diminish in the future when the plans have been in force long enough for participants to obtain maximum pension benefits which require ten years of contributions. At age seventy or over, a participant may draw Canada or Quebec Pension benefits whether or not he continues to work.

Maximum monthly payments after five years of contributions to these universal pension plans are $55.00 per month, and were available at the end of 1970. There is an escalator clause which permits annual increases to a maximum of 2 percent per year. This means, in effect, that the cost of living must rise by 2 percent or more for the increase to go into effect. In 1976, when the plans have been in effect for ten years, those participants who have reached age sixty-five and have contributed for ten years will be able to draw $110.00 per month plus any annual increases occurring in the next five years.

With the assurance of some pension income, inability to qualify for participation in a private pension plan becomes less serious. Similarly, the argument, used by many employers in the past that they did not wish to hire older workers in order to avoid the embarrassment and adverse publicity which could arise if an employee were retired without adequate pension, can now be dealt with effectively.

The success of these various efforts is greatly enhanced by activities in the voluntary sector. At the national level, we have worked closely with the Canadian Welfare Council and its Division on Aging. Golden Age clubs and other activities for older people are expanding rapidly and the establishment of pre-retirement courses under adult education programs is becoming more frequent. We think that these initiatives are offsetting to some extent the traditional concept that all old people are infirm, are dependent and require care. As older workers become more involved in the planning and implementation of their own programs and services of recreation and education, they are emerging as a dynamic group of varied talents who have much to contribute to society.

Chapter 15

UNITED STATES GOVERNMENT EMPLOYMENT PROGRAMS FOR THE MIDDLE-AGED

CHARLES E. ODELL

The Office of Systems Support has responsibility for designing about two and a quarter billion dollars' worth of manpower programs for the Manpower Administration including everything except the modified technical services of the old United States Employment Service such as counseling, testing, occupational analysis, and a few other services that are presumed to be supportive of the mainstream of the Manpower programs.

Several years ago we conceived the idea that we needed to develop an on-going concern in the field of aging, centering on the role of the practitioners in developing, supporting, creating, and innovating programs and services directed to finding solutions to the problems of middle-aged and older workers who, for reasons usually not of their own making, are confronted with the necessity for a change of employment in what is essentially a hostile and rather bewildering environment in the job market. Whereas a significant amount of money, at least in relative terms, has been invested in the general field of aging and in the field of retirement, and in the field of health related to retirement, and whereas every knowledgeable person in the field talks about preventive measures anticipatory of the problems of debilitation and decline in old age, there is very little central effort and money directed specifically at discovering and promoting those preventive measures. Those preventive measures, in my judgment, should focus primarily upon the need of middle-aged workers for a continuing useful, creative and productive role in society. That is what the National Institute of Industrial Gerontology is all about.

The purpose of our seminars is to bring together key people from national, regional, and state-local levels in the employment security system to discuss the latest findings and information and expertise in the field of industrial gerontology, that is, in the field of creative utilization, readjustment, and placement of the middle-aged and older worker.

This involves exploration of what industry is doing or is not doing; what labor thinks and is doing; what government is doing or should be doing about the problems of the middle-aged and older worker, and to share this information and expertise with those who are trying to help middle-aged and older workers find jobs. The staff specialists who attend our meetings have the job of interpreting to staff, clients and supervisors what it is that is special and what it is that is promising and what it is that is discouraging about the problems and prospects of middle-aged and older persons.

People like myself have a kind of duality of career interests and concern for middle-aged and older workers. To demonstrate the difficulty in its most sophisticated form: when I filled out papers for the Executive Development Program of the United States Civil Service Commission and identified a career interest in the general area of social gerontology, the papers came back with a statement that there were no codes in their system which appropriately reflected this particular skill or experience. There was also a little note attached, to the effect that we would never have a call for such a thing anyway so why worry. Government has staked out big claims in this field and there are presumed to be people all over the government who are working in the field of aging. Secretary Finch has testified before a Congressional Committee about the billions of dollars we are spending on older people, yet there is apparently no place in the Executive Career Development System which recognizes the need for specialized skills in this area.

I don't have a formal accredited claim to such skills like some of my colleagues in this area. I only have about twenty years of substantive practical experience in the field and, therefore, I really don't have an academic claim to pursue. But the fact remains that specialists in social gerontology would have equal problems in staking out a claim under the present Civil Service classification. That should bother all of us a little bit. Perhaps that ought to be the number one project for the Gerontological Society, which presumably is interested in training people for this field and getting them into the right places in government.

These remarks are tangential, but they do illustrate a point. In the press of the times and in the milieu of the Manpower Administration and the Department of Labor of the past several years, it is very difficult to maintain a steady, forward thrust in doing something about the employment problems of middle-aged and older people. It is not only in the employment area that we have difficulty in developing a sense of obligation to action and concern for the older part of our population.

Essentially, the problem from the point of view of the dynamics of the labor force and the pressures that we face in trying to develop an overall manpower policy and strategy really springs from the surfacing of an old and persistent truth. Youth unemployment among black and Spanish-speaking people is running at twice the rates for whites and, beyond that, the rate of youth unemployment generally is running at twice that of adult unemployment. In addition, during the last ten years people of middle and late middle-age have had comparatively low rates of unemployment. They are the experienced workers, in demand in an active economy. Those who look at these unemployment rates as the criterion for determining where priorities should be set are eternally asking why we worry about the older worker when he seems to be doing pretty well.

To be sure, we have to be concerned about the blacks and Spanish-speaking young people who are a great challenge to our program. I remember very well sitting down with the Assistant Secretary of Labor for Manpower and Employment after the Department of Labor had just published a book about the

Negro family. I asked how it was that he was so concerned with this problem but didn't seem to care about the problem of the middle-aged or older persons. He responded by saying in effect "Well, I don't see any older people out here picketing, I don't see any older people out here threatening to tear down the establishment." At that point I had been through fifty or sixty rallies on Medicare where, by the simple process of organization and outreach, we could produce a crowd of 7,500 to fifteen thousand older and retired people at the drop of a hat.

But the truth is that these pressures from the young underprivileged group prevail and continue to concern the political leadership of the country, particularly in the Executive Branch. In the Legislative Branch it is a slightly different problem. Several pieces of legislation affecting older people got little attention in the press but when they came to a vote they carried with close to unanimous support in both Houses of Congress. Medicare might be regarded as the exception, but let us remember that Medicare never came to a vote in the House of Representatives until it was finally enacted into law in 1965. It came to a vote only once in the Senate before it was finally passed and that was on such an abortive basis that it cannot be regarded as typical of the general fate of legislation for older people.

The significant thing is that when the Older Americans Act, which the Johnson Administration opposed, came to a vote in the House, it passed with one dissenting vote. It went to the Senate and was unanimously passed, went back to the House and was unanimously adopted there with conference amendments based on the Senate action. So it may be that the Executive Branch of the Government, in this regard, at least, is not really tuned in to what is going on in the country and how those who are taking the pulse of the American people feel about the problems and needs of older Americans.

I can play a numbers game with you to illustrate the point. If I say three, eight, two, four, three, six, it does not really mean anything to you, but if I say 38–24–36, you know I am talking about the male's ideal of the female configuration. Now, if I apply the same kind of numbers game to the politics on aging it goes something like 45, 55, 30 which suggests a very peculiar female silhouette, but profound political insight. Fifty-five percent of the total vote in this country is registered by people over forty-five years of age and yet those forty-five and over constitute only 30 percent of the population. My point is that despite the youth orientation in the culture, the votes are still with the older population. That may not be true indefinitely. Reducing the voting age to eighteen may change the picture. But I'm told that even in the States where the voting age is below eighteen there is still a very low rate of voting participation among the younger people. I keep coming back to this point, in dealing with administrators, managers, practitioners, the people on the firing line, that we have a responsibility to work more effectively with the middle-aged and older person. This is not a matter of preference, an "either/or." It is a matter of balance and sound policy in a democratic society. At this point in the history and growth of the national manpower program the function of the National Institute of Industrial Gerontology is to keep this issue and concern alive.

Last November I testified before the Senate Special Committee on Aging on what the Department of Labor and the Manpower Administration were doing for middle-aged and older people. All I really had to talk about that was new, different, significant, and relevant was the work that we were doing under our contract with the National Institute of Industrial Gerontology.

We started out in the Institute by commissioning a series of working papers on new developments in the field of Industrial Gerontology. In order to be sure that that effort was relevant and meaningful we called together a group of distinguished people in the field of aging and particularly people experienced in the employment and retirement aspects of aging. The papers in the curriculum guide resulted from those discussions.

Once the curriculum was developed, we pretested it with a representative group of State Employment Security Administrators. Following that, we made a formal test of the curriculum with the practitioners. The first meeting involved the states of the New England region with the cooperation of the University of New Hampshire Regional Council for New England. This was a very successful meeting, and one in which I think the practitioners had a chance, for the first time, to talk back and tell us whether we were on the right track. The Annapolis meeting was the second in the series of meetings with state and local office people, and we hope to continue through the remainder of next year with the central, the southwestern, and the northwestern states in similar regional institutes.

Basic education and orientation, sharing the new ideas and the new developments, are only one part of the Institute's program. Another part is related to the whole business of stimulating what I might call action-oriented experimentation and demonstration at the level where the problem is. We try to develop local interest among key people from labor, management, the employment service, the universities, and other interested community groups in defining and solving a problem which is bothering them. Having defined the problem and designed an approach to studying it, the group would then seek funding from a variety of sources to carry out a demonstration or an action-oriented research program to find solutions.

A specific example has to do with sharpening up our abilities to appraise, diagnose and predict the physical and psychological capacity of older workers to adjust to change in the employment world. Our model is the Koyl system now in use in de Haviland Aircraft, Ltd. in Toronto, Canada. We are funding the Maine State Employment Security agency to apply the Koyl system to a sample of unemployed middle-aged and older workers to see what happens when you follow those people longitudinally into the job market for a given period of time. The study will look not only at the effectiveness of the techniques of appraisal but also at their practicality for use in manpower programs. In another state we are attempting to develop a detailed training program for practitioners on the job, not only for the employment service but also for cooperating agencies such as Vocational Rehabilitation, Welfare, and the Community Action Agencies. This is being conducted by the Minnesota Employment Security Agency. We are considering other promising areas for operational research and demonstration. How can we really stimulate on-going interest in the whole concept of the second careers for middle-aged and older people, not only for those who need to work for the extra income, but for those who need to work for psychological and social reasons?

One question that arises is "What ever happened to the older worker specialists? What happened to the emphasis on specialized job counseling, job development, placement, and follow-up services for middle-aged and older people as a thrust of the Department of Labor and particularly of the Manpower Administration and the Employment Service?" Well, we are going through a major organizational and conceptual revolution in the design and implementation of manpower services. In the process the older worker program has been given short shrift for the reasons I have already mentioned. However, in spite of these temporary setbacks, there are approaches that can make a contribution not only to defining better the older worker's needs but to doing something to see that his needs are fulfilled.

For example, we fund $41 million worth of Operation Mainstream programs, most of which are targeted on middle-aged and older workers. In most of those programs the guidelines say that the people who are to be enrolled in Mainstream shall be recruited by, and certified by, the public employment service as being appropriate for inclusion in the program. We don't know how effectively and universally that guideline has been implemented. In some places it has been implemented rather faithfully, in others rather loosely. Another aspect of the program is that, beyond the initial recreation and conservation emphasis which characterized the first year of operation, it has become increasingly a senior citizens' community-service corps type of program. The people recruited are supposed to be placed in public service employment designed to contribute something to the welfare and betterment of the community. Now I see a logical and meaningful use of Mainstream volunteers within the Manpower system itself. Every Mainstream project ought to have a corps of from five to ten paid workers

assigned to work at the employment service in the extension
of placement and recruitment and follow-up activities for other
older people. We did two experimental and development proj-
ects: one in Louisville, Kentucky and one in Sacramento, California that proved that with a limited professional staff and
a corps of senior volunteers who were paid, not wages but
only out-of-pocket expenses, it was possible to reach more than
a thousand people fifty-five and over, two thirds of whom had
never heard of the public employment service, and to place
about half of those who were reached in continuing part-time
and full-time jobs. Thus, with expenditures for one professional
and a handful of volunteers, it was possible to extend the influence of the employment service to middle-aged and older
people in those two communities on quite an effective basis.

Let us also recall some simple realities that we, in the Manpower programs, are confronted with. I don't know of anybody
who is more disadvantaged than the middle-aged black or
older black who is living in a kind of triple jeopardy. He is
old, black, and poor. Second, I don't know of anybody who is
more disadvantaged than an older worker who by virtue of a
change in the economy, or in the reorganization or relocation
of his company, has been thrown out of a job and left with
no place to go. If his disadvantage is not immediately apparent, it is largely because he has unemployment insurance benefits for a while and some savings and resources on which he can
draw. However, his disadvantage becomes readily apparent
just a few months down the road.

It is too easy for us to shift gears and move away from this
pervasive problem in our society. If we have to improvise
and pull things together and work them in different forms to
get the job done, that is probably what we are being paid for.
If we don't do this it is largely because it is too easy to sit
back and say "Well these guys in Washington have changed
their minds; they don't believe in the older worker any more."
As far as I am personally concerned and as far as my office
is concerned, and I hope, eventually as far as the new Manpower Administration is concerned, *we have not abandoned
our interest and our concern and our dedication to the idea*

that middle-aged and older people are the backbone of the American labor force. They are clearly the backbone of the voting population, clearly an asset which needs to be conserved and utilized and not thrown on the scrap heap. In one way or another with the help of the older-worker specialists, and with the help of the National Council on Aging, and with the help of our friends in related professional spheres of interest such as the Gerontological Society, we aim to keep this issue alive; we aim to keep this program going; we aim to find ways in which to accommodate and to effect more of a thrust for middle-aged and older people in the basic manpower delivery systems.

I should mention one other major development. We are currently experimenting in ten cities with a new basic delivery system for manpower services, which strives for balance with individualized emphasis, to help all job seekers in accordance with their basic needs. The system encourages the job-ready to gain access to the system through self-service. Dr. Harold Sheppard and his colleague, A. Harvey Belitsky, did a study of job-seeking behavior of unemployed workers in Erie, Pennsylvania seven or eight years ago which showed that the job-seekers who did the best, *regardless of age,* were the ones who were motivated to seek work aggressively for themselves, not the ones who were waiting for the intervention of a third party to initiate the action. From the basic concept we are working to design a level of service for the so-called job-ready (the skilled and experienced, regardless of age) which focuses on their ability to help themselves. We try to give them all the information we have about where the jobs and training opportunities are. We expect the newly installed Job Bank System to provide much useful and easily understandable information to these job seekers.

A second area of service is for those who need some kind of help in the field of job development and selective placement. Many older workers need this kind of assistance.

The third area of service concentrates on those who really have no skills, no training, no meaningful work experience and who need extensive work training and work experience in order to become competitively employable. I am hoping that, in this new three-level configuration which we are trying in ten cities and which we will carefully study and evaluate, there is a place for the older worker specialist, the handicapped specialist, the youth specialist, and other people who work with special groups but who work with them in the context of a total delivery system that makes it possible for those with the greatest needs to get the greatest help. My judgment is that the kind of manpower system that will emerge from what we are now doing will be a very different system from the one we have had in the past.

As a final note to emphasize that point, let me tell you that if the Family Assistance Act is passed it will require fifteen thousand additional interviewers, counselors, job coaches and paraprofessional aides in the employment service system. That is a very big challenge. What it means is that we are going to have to develop a totally new approach to recruitment, training, and the orientation and employment of staff. I could say, for example, that we really don't have a problem about what to do with many of the enrollees in the Work Incentive program (WIN), because they could be working for us as paraprofessionals a year or two from now. That is the best source I can think of for recruiting the kind of people we need. It could be that many middle-aged WIN clients could also be recruited and trained to run the expanded child care program required under FAP.

These are very exciting, very challenging, and sometimes very confusing, times in Washington. The confusion is not a matter of not knowing where we want to go. The confusion centers on how best to implement the hypothesis, now seemingly a matter of policy, that it is preferable for people to work rather than to go on drawing welfare benefits. And if they have to work on a publicly supported payroll that is better than simply paying them to remain idle. Many people would reject this plan as unfeasible and unnecessary in a free economy. I think however, that they would agree that the economy cannot afford to dump large numbers of people on the basis of age or anything else and to expect at the same time to maintain its productivity and stability and economic health. I think the times are exciting, the challenge is great, the opportunity is unlimited, if only we have the perseverance to stick with it. I think in the ultimate configuration there is a significant role for middle-aged and older people and a significant opportunity for improving services to them.

NAME INDEX

Aiken, M., 10, 144
Anderson, B., 142
Anderson, J.E., 119
Antonovsky, Aaron, 160
Axlebank, Rashelle G., v, 17, 18

Bailey, Stephen, 187, 190
Barfield, Richard E., v, 45, 144
Barry, John R., 155
Becker, Gary, 34
Becker, Howard S., 167
Belbin, E., 143
Belbin, R.M., 143
Belitsky, A.H., 7
Bell, B., 121, 123
Bell, Daniel, 163
Bendiner, Robert, 187
Berger, Joseph, 142
Berkowitz, Bernard, 99, 115
Berkowitz, Monroe, v, 169
Birren, James E., 141
Bixby, Lenore E., 24
Botwinick, 134, 141
Brazer, H.E., 154
Break, G.F., 33
Breen, Leonard Z., 141
Brennan, Michael, 176, 177
Brooks, George W., 87
Butler, R.W., 8

Campbell, Ian, v, 192
Caplow, Theodore, 164
Child, Josiah, 32
Chown, S., 134
Cobb, Sidney, v, 12, 87
Cohen, Albert K., 144
Cohen, W.J., 154
Connelly, Winnifred E., 87
Corning, Peter A., 189

Damon, A., 121, 123
David, M.H., 154

Douglas, Paul H., 32
Droege, R.C., 119
Duesenberry, James, 33
Durand, John D., 35

Eells, K., 121, 124, 137
Egge, Karl, 66
Epstein, Lenore A., 45, 46

Ferman, L.A., 10, 144
Flaim, Paul O., 22
Fleisler, Belton M., 66
Franke, Walter H., 144
Friedmann, E.A., 144
Form, W.H., 144, 163, 164
Forsyth, Gordon, 166
Fozard, James L., v, 117, 128, 132
Franco, S.C., 168
Froman, Lewis A., Jr., 187

Green, Russel F., v, 99, 115
Greenberg, Leon, vi, 42
Gripe, R.P., 159
Gross, Bertram, 187
Gross, Edward, 164

Haber, Lawrence D., vi, 141, 145, 146, 150, 154
Hamel, H.R., 161
Harris, Richard, 187
Havighurst, R.J., 144
Hays, W.L., 133
Heron, S., 134
Hirt, M.L., 119

Jaffe, A.J., 20, 143, 163
Johnson, Clarence G., 173

Kadushin, Charles, 160
Kasl, Stanislav V., vi, 87
Kegan, Paul, 154
Kerloz, George A., 169

211

King, H.F., 175
Kohen, Andrew I., 66
Kossoris, Max D., 175
Kreps, Juanita M., vi, 31, 32, 37

Lazarsfeld, Marie Jahoda, 90
Lecht, Leonard, 41
London, Routledge, 154
Long, Clarence D., 33, 36
Loomba, R.P., 10
Lowe, J.C., 163

Malinovsky, M.R., 155
Malthus, T.R., 32
McClelland, David, 11
Mechanic, David, 160
Meeker, M., 121, 124, 137
Merton, Robert K., 144
Meyer, Jack A., vi, 63
Miljus, Robert C., 66
Miller, D.C., 164
Moore, J.W., 163
Moore, Wilbert E., 31, 164
Morgan, James, 45, 58, 144, 154
Morse, Nancy C., 144
Murray, Janet H., 46

Neugarten, Bernice L., 163, 165, 167
Nosow, S., 144, 163, 164
Nuttall, Ronald L., vi, 117, 128, 132

Odell, Charles E., vi, 119, 199

Parnes, Herbert S., vi, 63, 65, 66, 77
Petroni, F.A., 166

Ravin, L.H., 145, 163
Reimanis, Gunars, vi, 99
Riley, Matilda White, 175

Rings, E. Eleanor, 24
Rose, C.L., 121, 123
Rusalem, Herbert, 164

Sauvy, Alfred, 9
Schmidt, Ronald M., 66
Schuchat, Theodor, vii
Schupack, M.B., 143, 176, 177
Shackle, G.L.S., 32
Sheldon, Eleanor B., 164
Sheppard, Harold L., vii, 5, 7, 10, 11, 144
Slavick, Fred, 144
Slote, Alfred, 87
Smith, Adam, 32
Smith, Richard T., 145
Spengler, Joseph J., 32
Spitz, Ruth S., 66
Sprague, Norman, ix

Taeuber, Irene B., 35
Taft, Philip, 176, 177
Tibbitts, Clark, 141, 189
Townsend, Peter, 154

Voss, Justin, 40

Wachtel, H., 10
Warner, W.L., 121, 124, 137
Weiss, R.S., 144
Welford, A.T., 141, 143
Wickenden, E., 188
Wilcock, Richard C., 144
Wilensky, Harold L., 38
Williams, Arthur C., Jr., 177
Winston, Gordon C., 35
Withers, Irma, vii, 13

Zelditch, M., Jr., 142

SUBJECT INDEX

A

Accident rates, 174
Activities, postretirement, 56
Adult Occupational Training Act, 195
"Advance to new problems," 191
Age discrimination in Employment Act, 17
Age discrimination, increased, 64
Age-Intelligence relationship, 99–116
Age-mean scale scores, 101T, 102T, 103T
Age norms, 165
Ageism, 8
Aging process, biological decrements of, 141
Anxiety, job interview, 11
Atherosclerosis, 120
Attainment, educational, 6
Attitude factors, 76, 77T

B

Birth control, 5
Birth rate, low
  effect of, 13
  forecasting of, 15
Blood pressure, 89, 90

C

Canada Manpower Centres, 193
Canada, older workers in, 192–198
Capacity losses, 153, 154T
Cellular maturation, 142
Cholesterol, changes in, 89, 90
Colds, 91
Current Population Survey, 65, 66
Curve, labor supply, 32
  inelastic, 33

D

Death control, 5
"Debating the proposals," 189

Decision-making, retirement, 57–59
Dependency ratio, 6, 16
Devaluation, age and capacity, 141–168
"Diffuse status characteristics," 142
Disability
  definition of, 146
  occupation at onset of, 158T
  prevalence of, 148, 149T
  severity of, 155T
Disabling condition, major, 147
Disassemble test, 128
"Discretionary work," 40
Disorders, cardiovascular, 153

E

Education, 9, 161
Ego resilience, level of, 89
"Emergence of need," 189
Employment experience, recent, 72–74
Employment patterns, industrial, changes in, 18–19
Employment programs, 199–209
Environment
  caretaking of, 44
  "oldsoldiers," 114
"Execution of policy," 190

F

Free time, growth of, 33
"Full income," 34
Full-scale I.Q., 100
Functional limitations index, 156, 157T

G

General Aptitude Test Battery, xiii, 117–138
  implications of, 135–137
  need for, 118
  scores, 127, 130T, 131T
"Generative change," 188

213

Gerontology
  definition of, ix
  industrial contributions to, 5–12
  institutional analysis, 7

H

Health problems, serious, 54, 64, 69–72, 82, 83
Heart disease, coronary, 90
Hypertension, 90, 91

I

Income incentives, 32
Income vs. leisure, note on, 42–45
Institute for Social Research, 47
Intellectual decline, 112
International Union–UAW, 46
Intestinal flu, 91

J

Joblessness, long-term, 21

K

Koyl System, 204

L

Labor force
  comparison by colors, 79T, 80T
  comparison of, 69T, 73T
  dropouts from, 22–23
  participation, 151T
    decline in, 5
  withdrawal from, 63–86
Laziness, administrative, 9
Leisure
  definition of, 40
  inelastic demand for, 34
  lost, 38
  temporally concentrated, 39
Leisure-time patterns, variations in, 36
Limitations, functional, 147
"Lump-of-Labor" theory, 33
Lump-of-leisure theory, 37, 39

M

Manpower Development and Training Act, 9

Manpower needs, declining, 17
Motivation, 11

N

National Institute of Gerontology, 200
National Safety Council, 175
Nomograph, 124, 126T, 127T
  structural factors, 128

O

Occupational Aptitude Pattern Structures, 118
Occupational patterns, changes in, 19–20
Office of Systems Support, 197
Operation Mainstream, 205

P

Participation, household, 148, 153T
Pension plans, private
  age discrimination in, 24
  growth in, 18, 24
Pensions, portable, 94
Peptic ulcer, 91
Performance I.Q., 100
Performance requirements, 157
Planning, retirement, effect on, 48
Population
  age distribution of, 14 fig., 15 fig.
  maturing of, 15
Premiums, formula pure, 178
Progressive Matrices Test, 134

R

Rate, re-employment, 7
  factors of, 10
Retired, income of, 51–52
Retirement
  early, 6, 23, 45–59
  factors of, 47–49
  satisfaction with, 55
  threshold level of, 48
  voluntary, 81–82
Retirement-income-maintenance programs, 46

S

Self-image, 11
Seniority, 164
SES, level, 119
 estimating of, 120
Skill obsolescence, rate of, 64
Social activity, 148, 153T
Social identification, 144
Social Security Administration, 46
Standard Metropolitan Statistical Areas, 65
Stress, environmental, 142
Subsequent injury funds, 180
 problems of, 181–182
Suicides, 90

T

Technology, changes in, 18
"Tenure," 164
Tests, functional, 9
Time, allocation of, 35
"Time for decisive action," 190

U

Unemployment
 duration of, 26T
 education and, 21
 medical aspects of, 87–96
 medical impact of, 12
 pattern of, 26T

United States Employment Service, 7
Uric acid, level of, 89, 90

V

Verbal I.Q., 100

W

Wage rates, 32
Warner system, 121, 122T
 categories of, 138
Wechsler Adult Intelligence Scale, 99, 100
 test results, 106T, 107T, 108T, 110T, 111T
Wechsler-Bellevue, 100
Welfare, economic, 52
Withdrawal, temporary, 84
Work and Play, lifetime tradeoffs between, 31–41
Work experience, lifetime, 74, 75T
Work Incentive Program, 208
Work, nature of, 159
Worker, older
 legislative trends affecting, 187–191
 position of, 17–27
 unemployment of, 20–21
Workmen's Compensation, 169–184
 insurance pricing, 177
 origins and purposes, 172–173
 trends in, 173